THE PORTAL TO PAST LIFE
Insight

Lynn C. LeBlanc,
Clinical Certified Hypnotherapist, Master Hypnotist, Reiki Master, B.Comm. and B.Educ.

◆ FriesenPress

Suite 300 - 990 Fort St
Victoria, BC, Canada, V8V 3K2
www.friesenpress.com

Copyright © 2015 by Lynn C. LeBlanc
First Edition — 2015

All rights reserved.

No part of this publication may be reproduced in any form, or by any means, electronic or mechanical, including photocopying, recording, or any information browsing, storage, or retrieval system, without permission in writing from FriesenPress.

ISBN
978-1-4602-7760-7 (Hardcover)
978-1-4602-7761-4 (Paperback)
978-1-4602-7762-1 (eBook)

1. Psychology, Hypnotism

Distributed to the trade by The Ingram Book Company

TABLE OF CONTENTS

Dedication v
Preface 1
Introduction 7
Chapter 1: Choices Made – Opportunities Missed 11
Chapter 2: Whose Journey Is it Anyway? 17
Chapter 3: Past and Present Connections 23
Chapter 4: Holding In a Long Forgotten Secret 31
Chapter 5: Screams In the Night 41
Chapter 6: Stuck in the Details 51
Chapter 7: Sometimes Things Are Not What They Appear 57
Chapter 8: Teachers Come In Strange Disguises 67
Chapter 9: Karmic Debt 73
Chapter 10: Soul Mates 83
Chapter 11: Unanswered Prayers 93
Chapter 12: Now What? 107
Appendix 109
   Worksheets: Getting Started 109
      Exercise 1: Your Beliefs 110
      Exercise 2: Patterns in Your Life 113

Exercise 3: Accessing Your Subconscious 117
Exercise 4: Possible Past Lives 119
Exercise 5: Finding Someone to Help 122
About the Author 125

DEDICATION:

I believe there are people who come into our lives when we get off our path. They give us a kick in the butt to get us moving in the right direction once again.

This book is dedicated to Katrina who knew the proper boot to use for the job – one of heartfelt support and encouragement.

Thank you!

PREFACE:

In my mind's eye I saw a young boy sitting on the shores of the Amazon.

He had finished his chores for the day, but if he went back to the village, his grandfather would find something else for him to do. So here he sat.

A light breeze off the river cooled the intense summer heat. This spot was the perfect place for a relaxing break. And he knew exactly how to spend it.

He hooked a small piece of food to a line and dropped it into the river – but he wasn't fishing. As quick as the tasty morsel hit the water, he tugged it back out. When it got an inch or two above the water, I could see the game he was playing. Small piranhas jumped out of the water trying to catch the bait. The boy was toying with them.

As I relayed the images I saw to my client, she stared at me in disbelief.

She had come to my office in hopes of receiving information about her past lives. Was hearing she actually had a past life, too much for her? Or was it because she was once male?

I sat silent, waiting for her to speak.

"I have lived in northern Canada all my life," she began. "But when I was young, my brother's best friend had a fish tank. In the tank he had piranhas. I remember spending hours beside that tank.

My favorite thing was to dangle a piece of meat over the tank and watch those silly little fish jump."

Can you believe that? In a different time, in a different life, she played the exact same game. And really – pet piranhas in Canada?

Now it was my turn to be shocked.

This was when I realized there was more to reviewing past lives then even *I* had thought.

REINCARNATION OR WORM FOOD?

Heaven or Hell. Paradise or eternal damnation. Spin the wheel to determine your fate.

What is reincarnation and how does the whole concept of death and rebirth work?

The concept of reincarnation is a question individuals, cultures, and religions have debated for centuries. On an individual level, the answer is important because it provides hope – reassurance that death is not the end. Reassurance that one's spirit will continue to another life and not be restricted to a limited number of years. This is especially important if one believes this limited life determines if they are worthy enough to go to 'heaven' – or unworthy and damned to 'hell'.

If we could find *the answer* to the question of reincarnation, we could in essence address two profound issues that haunt many individuals, if not all of human kind: fear of the unknown and fear of screwing up with the accountable lasting an eternity.

Fear of the unknown – in this case, death. What happens when we die? Where do we go? Does it hurt? Then what...? The mind – and worse the imagination – can come up with some creative versions of heaven and some horrific versions of hell and everything in-between. Most horror stories and movies capitalize on subjecting the audience to the unknown – the longer, the better. By prolonging the uncertainty, the creator intensifies the feelings to an ultimate climax of adrenaline for the audience. This can sometimes last for days or longer, creating nightmares, or even physical trauma such as stomach aches, headaches, etc.

> As H.P. Lovecraft stated, "The oldest and strongest emotion of mankind is fear, and the oldest and strongest kind of fear is fear of the unknown."
> (*Supernatural Horror in Fiction*)

So what is the relief for this fear? Knowledge. Knowing what the evil is diminishes the anxiety. Like a pressure valve, knowledge releases the fear – until the next time something unknown increases the pressure once again. When the audience knows what the characters are facing, the knowing may not eliminate the fear, but it does take a lot of bite out of fear's bark.

Therefore, if in fact, we do come back again and again – to live life after life – the knowledge of that fact could significantly decrease our anxiety and fear of death. Fear of being eaten by worms, fear of a black emptiness, fear of the unknown.

Knowing we have had past lives, we can infer the cycle will continue and we will live again in the future. We will know a part of us – our consciousness, essence, soul, spirit, or whatever you wish to call it – a part of us goes on. If this knowledge does nothing else, it gets us past the idea of simply being worm food.

The knowledge that a part of us goes on also helps with our second fear of screwing up in one life and paying for that mistake for eternity. There are many individuals with the perspective that they have one life, *one* chance to get into heaven. Some find it very difficult to make and stick to decisions. They try to follow each choice through to all possible outcomes, and rate their odds, but become almost paralyzed to make the 'wrong' choice. What if something does not go as planned, and something bad happens, and it is their fault?

To make matters worse – we don't know the rules. What are we responsible for? If we get a job that someone else needed to provide for their family, does that mean we did something wrong? If we get the top marks in high school and someone else commits suicide because they didn't, are we damned forever? What if we did something stupid when we were a kid? Is that it? What if we spend the rest of our life trying to make amends – does that count?

Understandably, we would find some relief in knowing there are several chances to make amends. Since humans seem to be their own worst critic, sometimes we may even feel it will take lifetimes of making amends to release the blame we put on ourselves. The knowledge that we might have more time gives us hope.

Other individuals with the one life perspective have difficulty living with choices they have made or which they believe have been made for them. The choices of career, spouse, family relationships, or having children are often viewed as exclusionary choices. If you choose one path, you cannot choose the corresponding opposite – although some try. For example, when one relationship does not seem to be working, they get rid of it and find another. Remember, they believe you only have a limited amount of time to find happiness. How many careers can you have in one life? And how many people say they regrettably chose the wrong one?

If there is only one life to experience everything – what would you choose? How upset would you be if you never, ever got to experience holding your own child? Never! For some that is a physical reality, a very painful physical reality.

It is incredible to see how the stress of *what could have been* weighs on an individual – physically, mentally, emotionally, and spiritually. However, with the knowledge of multiple lives, the hope for that experience is still alive.

What would it be like to say, "That's okay. I can have children in my next life." Or "That's okay. I had a dozen in my last life." Again, the pressure to pack everything into one life is gone.

Researching reincarnation to alleviate some of these fears and bring hope for chances to do things differently was one of my main inspirations for this book. However, as I progressed through the journey, I found there is so much more involved in reviewing past lives, so many more benefits.

As a hypnotherapist, the sessions I have depicted in this book show me, and hopefully you, the importance of past life exploration. The knowledge of these lives and the content within can profoundly affect one's current life and experiences, as well as ease many fears. I hope you find some connection with these individuals and can share in the sense of peace they discovered through their personal journeys.

INTRODUCTION:

Before we begin, it might be beneficial to have a basic understanding of how one can access the information trapped within past lives.

There are two general methods I use to travel back to a previous life and retrieve information. The first method is hypnosis.

Hypnosis is controversial. The reason it's controversial is because even though hypnosis has been around for centuries, people still don't really know how it works. The human mind is that proverbial black box that eludes our understanding.

When hypnosis is used for reducing stress or anxiety, science tends to explain successful results by examining physical changes. If a person thinks happy thoughts, blood pressure and certain chemicals in the body are often reduced. Hence the feeling of anxiety decreases, for example.

However, when it comes to using hypnosis to access information in the mind, it is more difficult to explain scientifically. So the old adage "seeing is believing" comes into play.

This is especially true if the information cannot be somehow validated. The retrieval of information such as an address is easy to assess. That is not the case with past life memories.

The benefits of exploring past lives, however, can be seen. Benefits like decreased pain, the disappearance of phobias, increased feelings of self worth or self confidence, and improved relationships, are often results of past life reviews. These things can be physically seen and have a profound impact on quality of life.

It is for this reason, we explore past lives. If there are seeable benefits, the process of using hypnosis seems to be accepted – especially by those receiving the benefits.

So what is hypnosis?

Hypnosis is a process that induces a state of altered consciousness. This state of altered consciousness is often referred to as a trance. And a trance allows the subconscious mind to be open.

The subconscious is like a storage room. When it's open, you have access to what's inside. Everyone has their own room, and every room is different. The rooms are different because of what information we put inside them.

Everything you put in your specific room is taken from your specific world. This includes all your knowledge and experiences, in addition to all your values, beliefs, hopes, and fears. And most importantly, everything in that room is created from your specific perspective.

For example, two siblings recall going to the beach as young children. One remembers meeting friends and having a great day. The other remembers feeling ostracized by the group and having a horrible day. Even though they both participated in the same event, each had very different perspectives of the day. But regardless of their interpretation, the day was recorded, with all the individual thoughts and feelings, in each of the sibling's respective rooms.

It is not simply our unique life experiences that we store in our room. It's those experiences *plus* how they are colored by our individual values, beliefs, hopes, fears, and the life lessons we have chosen to learn.

Basically, that room contains everything that makes you – you.

In addition to putting things into our storage room, when our subconscious is open, we can also take things out. By opening the room and looking inside ,we could extract virtually any information about an individual.

The Portal To Past Life Insight

Don't panic!

Your storage room is locked, and you hold the key. In actuality, you hold the *keys*.

The room contains filing cabinets with various locks at various levels. There are locks on the main door, the individual cabinets, drawers, and even some files. The information within your subconscious is protected by your conscious and subconscious minds. That is why hypnosis works sometimes and not others, and on some people better than others.

Let's go back to the content of the room and how it relates to reincarnation.

If the room truly does contain everything that encompasses you, what about past lives? If we are an accumulation of experiences, wouldn't we have to include *all* our experiences? Regardless of where or when they took place?

This room, this part of your being – call it your subconscious, your spirit, soul, or something else – contains all that is you. This includes all your past life experiences. And it stores them. Forever.

Therefore if one wants to retrieve information from a past life, hypnosis is an incredible tool. It opens the doors and locks to allow access to your subconscious, which is where all the details of your past lives reside.

The most challenging part of hypnosis is getting past the stigma that is connected to its name. Like I mentioned, hypnosis is controversial. So even though trances have been used for centuries, the concept of inducing trances is still shrouded in history and mystery. Therefore, hypnosis is often misunderstood and feared.

Sometimes the use of trances is tied to witchcraft or unholy rituals. Other times information gained through the process is dismissed as unsubstantial or made-up. More recently, the word hypnosis is associated with parties and watching people do silly things in the guise of entertainment.

To effectively use hypnosis, all of these issues have to be addressed, and with each client. Remember each person has their own perspective, their own set of locks. So before I ever get to see a client's storage room, I have to be permitted into their house – into their mind.

Since hypnosis is the primary technique for retrieving past life information, to use it successfully you have to remember – the first step should be to dispel any myths about the process. The locks must be opened one at a time, working from the outside in.

Although the second technique I use is faster, I want to emphasize the significance of viewing your own past life first-hand. The impact on an individual is truly unforgettable. The experience itself, is often life altering.

That being said, for most individuals it takes numerous sessions to retrieve enough information and detail to analyze issues across multiple lifetimes. In the cases where more information or a complex analysis is desired, I use a different technique or a combination of the two.

The second technique I use to review a past life is a form of self-hypnosis. I put myself into a trance and connect to the individual's subconscious directly.

Let me tell you, if hypnosis is controversial, this technique is much more so. And being the logical, left-brain thinker that I am, it has taken a lot for me to acknowledge and declare my talent in this area. (The piranhas definitely helped.)

Without venturing into a side discussion about psychics and mediums, let's just say, I can access the past lives of individuals myself. Through this direct process, I can see exactly what took place and talk to the individuals involved. This makes it easy to gather information, and the details are extremely clear. As a result we can start the analysis and comparison of lives much sooner.

In spite of how the information is retrieved, the important part is what we do with the information we get. The purpose of the whole process is to help individuals understand their lives and hopefully, maybe, improve them.

CHAPTER 1:

CHOICES MADE – OPPORTUNITIES MISSED

As a hypnotherapist, I never know who will walk through my office door – or how much they will be changed when they leave.

Barb sat in my comfy, chocolate-colored chaise. Relaxed and at ease, she counted backwards, and I watched the transformation begin.

"What are you wearing?"

"I am wearing my little brown shoes and a pretty little dress with bright yellow flowers." As she spoke, her voice changed into a young child, shy but full of energy.

"Where are you, and what are you doing?"

"Like always, the wagon is too full to carry me. I am keeping up, but sometimes it's hard. I just wish I did not have a hole in the bottom of my shoe. It is much easier walking without them, but I have to look the part. It doesn't matter anyways. We're almost there. I can see the town ahead. Just a little further, and then I can get to work – you know I am here on official company business."

"What important business has brought such a young lady to town today?"

She thought about the question, but for some reason she could not remember.

"Maybe there is a clue in the wagon," I said. "Go take a look inside, and see if you can find something that will remind you of why you came to town today."

The wagon contained stacks of pamphlets and posters.

"Can you read? Can you tell me what they say?"

Barb lowered her face and shook her head, her voice filled with mortification as the truth hit her like a pie in the face. "I'm in a circus. It's all here in vivid color. There are clowns, a ringmaster, and a girl standing on horse – literally, I'm part of a traveling circus!"

Forgive me, but I couldn't help but chuckle. She was not amused.

Begrudgingly she read me the poster.

– THE CIRCUS IS COMING TO TOWN –
Animals from around the world!
Death Defying Feats of Bravery -
Never before seen.
The Weird and The Bizarre!
Two days only this Friday and Saturday
from noon to 8:00.
Come One, Come All!!

Where some might find being part of a circus an exciting prospect, Barb looked shocked.

She just continued to mutter, "Yup, I work in a circus!"

Barb was in her mid-fifties and loved to sing. As her life unfolded, the choices she made put any notion of a professional singing career in the back seat. Family came first, and providing for them was foremost in her life.

Over the years, Barb tried to keep involved with singing by joining the church choir and several small bands. But Barb lived on a farm with a massive garden, two children, two dogs, and a husband, and we all know, family life keeps mothers very busy.

As the years passed, the demands of motherhood became the fleeting moments a grandmother cherishes. Barb's wonderful family grew up, and time was suddenly there for her. Time for her to look back and rediscover her wants and dreams – and maybe even some regrets.

Barb had tried several times in her life to learn to play an instrument. She always thought it would enhance her stage performance. However, every time she tried, something else got in the way.

When Barb heard about using hypnosis to retrieve past skills, she figured this just might be the solution – and possibly her ticket to bigger things. She never dreamed what weird and bizarre things would be waiting as she ventured into the world of past life regression – she was on the brink of a life-altering journey.

Her next memory was spoken in a quiet whisper. "I lifted the side of the tent and very quietly crawled back stage. I would get in terrible trouble if I was caught up this late, but it was worth the risk just to hear her sing." In the excited little voice of the girl she now was, Barb went on to describe her favorite act in the whole circus.

As the crowd sat restlessly on the bench seats, a young lady with the prettiest royal blue dress stepped onto a large wooden box that had been set up as a stage. No one else seemed to notice her, but Barb held her breath, waiting for that first note. When the young lady finally opened her mouth, the sweetest sound came floating over the noise, and the audience fell silent. All eyes shifted to the source of the beautiful sound. All mouths closed to listen, and a serene hush came across the room.

I watched as Barb's closed eyes strained to open. Even in this trance state, I could see the big eyes of a child in awe. She listened for some time before she spoke again with tiny tears rolling down her cheeks. "This is when I knew, I would sing! One day I would be on stage, and everyone would come to hear me sing."

Barb went on to describe a life of determined pursuit. She did anything and everything to get her time in the spot light. And when I brought her to the next significant point of that life, she painted an incredible scene that still gives me goose bumps when I think of it.

As the floor lights came up, she found herself alone at center stage. The majestic, deep purple of her dress was so rich, it was embellished only by a row of tiny beads and sequins starting at her left shoulder that ran down and across the waistline and ended at her right hip. She wore a violet and white feather that stood out among the curls of her long chestnut hair. The outfit, from feather to shoes, accentuated her hourglass figure. She was utterly stunning.

The complete transformation that came over Barb brought tears to my eyes. When she spoke with such vivid details, I could see just how beautiful she was. As she continued, I was awestruck.

She described the large theater with a balcony in the back and private booths on the sides. She described the fancy seats of the front row and the individuals sitting in them, and then finally she addressed Barb's unspoken request.

"Is there a message you wish to tell Barb, which can help her in her current life?" I asked the singer Barb had once been.

In a sultry voice, the answer came. "Long ago I learned to play the piano, and only once did I play on stage. Instruments are great to know, but don't let them cheat you of what is truly important."

Barb grew quiet, but when she spoke, her words grew with momentum, "With a single verse, I can have this whole room laughing with joy or devastated to tears. With the power of my words, I control their very emotions. I can bring back memories of love or memories of loss. And as I stand here before them, I get to watch it all unfold. I take them on a journey through emotions of good and bad, and I get a front row seat. The music and the words are what are important. These two things are what move the audience."

Suddenly, she moved her hands like playing a piano, her closed eyes straining to see her fingers, concentrating on every move.

"When you have to watch an instrument – focus on what your fingers are doing, what notes come next – it takes away from the joy of the moment."

As she swooshed away the imaginary piano, she declared, "You *must* be in the moment! Your music will take them away. Enjoy the journey and watch them soar."

That powerful statement was the answer to Barb's question. It explained why she could not seem to focus or make time to learn to play an instrument. Deep down inside, she knew what was truly important – the music and the words.

After this epiphany, what more could we expect? But the journey was not over. I always take individuals through their death when we visit past lives. The reason is because as we die, we reflect on regrets and, in essence, set the stage for future lives. The passing contains insights that cannot be found anywhere else.

Sitting in a dimly lit room in a high backed chair, Barb's energy was slipping away. Her passing was close at hand. In a low whispery voice, she reflected on her life.

"It was a good life. I enjoyed my time and had everything I could ask for...money, fame, a beautiful house, and wonderful stages to sing on.

"Look at all my wonderful photos." Her arm made a wide arc. "They so capture my life. There, I was so young and impressionable in my little brown shoes and pretty little dress; and oh that stunning purple gown – how it made me feel so sexy and alive. That one is me in England. And there I danced in front of the Eiffel Tower in France."

Then in a heartbeat, the energy she gained from past memories melted away, "No other faces. Look at all my photos. There are no other faces in any of them, not one.

15

"I had friends along the way, but none lasted very long, not even long enough to stand in one photo. No loved ones. No family. No children. Not even a dog. And here I am at the end."

She took her final breath, and her essence left that body. "Do you want to know my biggest regret? I'm alone. I'm always alone."

As I brought the session to an end, and Barb came back to this time and place, I was surprised at what I saw – peace. There was an incredible sense of peace emanating from Barb.

"A giant weight I didn't know I was carrying has finally been lifted," she said.

People often wonder about the decisions they make, the paths they choose. What would their life have been like if they had spent more time and effort pursuing a talent, a dream? Well Barb now knew. She *had* that life. She had the body, the fame, and everything that went along with being a successful singer. And now she had the other: the family, the husband, the children, and even grandchildren. She had not totally deprived herself of the music, but it had not been her priority. This time her priority was having a family. Now, looking at the decisions she had made, she felt peace.

Barb left my office changed. She stood taller and more confident than I had ever seen her – as if she were still wearing those heels, that stunning purple dress, and a feather.

CHAPTER 2:

WHOSE JOURNEY IS IT ANYWAY?

"You're my last hope!" I hear this so often I want to say, "I'm not Obi-Wan Kenobi." But the voice on the phone once again sounds desperate; so I bite my tongue and respectfully listen.

It's funny how hypnotherapy always seems to be the last thing people try. And it's even funnier that they spend years trying other methods but want instant results from me. Good thing hypnosis and regression are so effective. Sometimes all they need is the missing piece of the puzzle, to see things from a different perspective.

Often we get stuck in the story. We can only see the particulars – our perception of a situation – and do not see the bigger picture. That was the case with Joan and her son Bradley. There was more to the situation than either of them realized.

"My son is not dumb," Joan said. "I don't care what they say. I know he's a smart kid. The system has failed him."

I heard the anguish in her voice. She described the home schooling, the tutors, the counsellors, and the psychologists. Everything from what he ate, to how long he slept, his friends, his lack of friends, his father, his mother, and now his parent's recent divorce. Every aspect of how she raised him became questioned as the cause of her son's issues.

What began as anguish changed to guilt and quiet remorse as she admitted, "Maybe they're right, maybe I failed him too.

"But it's not too late. I don't care what it takes. I know there is something that can be done, and I will find it. I will get him back on track!"

As a hypnotherapist, I look for the cause of the issue, so we don't just fix the symptoms. The symptoms are the particulars that are currently happening in an individual's life, and when you fix one symptom, another one often pops up to take its place. I want to find the cause: where did the issue originate – whatever *this* unwanted behaviour is – where and when did it come from?

"No one is dumb," I told her.

On the contrary many people labeled slow or having a learning disorder are some of the smartest people I have ever met. We just had to find the back story to the current situation. We needed the context to understand what was happening and then the *why* could be revealed.

I often find myself saying, "Go back to the cause. Let your subconscious take you where you need to be to see what you need to see. Go back to the time and place so you can find the key to the issue."

And as we went back, the story started to unfold.

He was such a happy boy. Running and playing with his friends. Times were hard, but his mother smiled with joy and hope as she looked at her only child. He meant the world to her. He was the only thing left of the man she once called husband. She would do anything for him.

One day the priests came to their village. Every few years, they came looking for those special children. The gods chose certain children to serve their earthly god, the pharaoh. It was an honor to have your child chosen. The parents were compensated, and the children were educated and taken to the palace for a life-long position as a scribe.

Scribes recorded the pharaoh's time on this earthly plain. They recorded all his accomplishments, battles, history, wives, and children. The pharaoh required this information to enter the afterlife.

Joan desperately wished this for her son.

As the priests entered the village, their attention was instantly drawn to one child in particular.

"The gods are truly with us today," remarked the youngest priest. "Even I can see how brightly that one's spark shines. He is very special indeed, and the pharaoh will be very pleased with our find."

Joan's heart beat quickly when she heard the priest's words. Who were they talking about? It took all Joan's courage to finally look up and see.

The priest's hand lay gently on her son's shoulder. Joan's dream began to unfold before her when they asked to be taken to his parents. She met the priest's gaze and knew. Joan and her son's lives would forever change.

Her son had been chosen.

He was the only child to be chosen from her village that year. And the very next day, the boy was taken away. His mother was very sad as she would likely never see her son again, but also very happy for the life he would now enjoy.

The boy was taught: taught to read and write, taught to listen and record, taught to cipher numbers and keep accounts. He was very smart and loved to learn.

He thrived in his new home and happily learnt everything they taught him. But then the teaching was over. His life was to change once again.

He was one of thirteen that had been collected from the area that season, but there were many who had come before and many who came after. Being of low birth, he was lucky to have been chosen at all. As a result, the role he was now destined to hold was, in fact, nothing like the one he or his mother expected.

Some older scribes attended the pharaoh's meetings and events, living very well in the palace. Other scribes had the responsibility to confer with the priests on what would be recorded, how, and where. They spent a lot of time with the priests and were also treated quite well. But this boy's role, like many others, was not as lavish and proved to be extremely mundane.

The boy spent twelve to fourteen hours a day at tables in a very small room with forty-nine other scribes – writing. When it got too dark, they used oil lamps, so they could continue – writing.

The material they received was only bits and pieces so they didn't even know what they were really writing about. Each scribe got a section to complete. As the sections were done the priests properly arranged the story. Like reading random paragraphs in a chapter, the scribes never saw the whole story. Sometimes the paragraphs were not even from the same book.

They were fed and given a place to sleep, and in return they wrote, and wrote, and wrote.

Hours turned into days, days into years, and years into his lifetime. And that was all.

As I remembered that boy in the village, I once again saw that vivid spark. The spark that had so easily pointed him out to the priests. The spark of that vibrant child. But now as he aged before my eyes, that spark slowly, painfully faded. All his potential, his dreams, and his life were fading from his expression. With silent tears flowing down my cheeks, I asked about the boy's death.

Within seconds, all I felt was a tremendous sense of peace from his spirit as it passed. In a very low, relieved voice, I heard his spirit say, "Freedom. Freedom from that room. Freedom from the pain of sitting, writing, constantly for my whole life. I was tied to that room, that table. No learning, no thinking. Only fragments of words, fragments of stories. No mental or physical activities, no sunlight, no life. It felt like eternity, and now – it's over."

The Portal To Past Life Insight

And with his last breath, the insight we were looking for finally came. "Never again."

As the past faded and the present came back into focus, I glanced over to Joan. There was no doubt to either of us that she was the mother in that life as well. She was the mother who gave up her son for a better life, and now she knew what that life had become.

As we sat and talked about Bradley's past life, everything began to take shape. The back story was now all there.

Even though the system had labelled him slow and stated he would always have trouble learning – Bradley was extremely smart. His spirit never again wanted to get trapped in a similar situation, and Bradley's subconscious knew that. Sitting behind a desk, staring at a computer day in and day out, was never going to be his fate in this life.

He enjoyed learning, his mom knew that, but he always seemed to try and hide it from her. When Joan home schooled him and used lots of hands-on learning techniques, physical props, and stories, he had done very well.

He enjoyed television but always seemed to get up and leave before the end of a program – almost like he was not allowed to see the whole story.

And he enjoyed being outside on their farm, but his mother always envisioned more for him.

Now comes the most interesting part of the story. I never met Bradley, only Joan. This was a past life reading I did for her, and as in this life, Bradley was an integral part. This was not Bradley's issue though. He really had it all worked out. This was all about Joan. This was *her* issue. Once she realized it was her dreams in the past that had led her son to that lonely, isolated life in ancient Egypt, things shifted.

Joan now realized she was doing the same thing in this life. She had dreams for her son. She wanted him to have a good education so he could get a good job, not realizing where it could lead.

Bradley's subconscious knew. He had found a perfect solution to never getting locked away again.

Several weeks later, I was happy to hear that Joan had found her son an apprenticeship program. The program would allow Bradley to work with his hands, meet people, and learn as he went from mentors and short, hands-on courses. Most importantly, Bradley would learn and progress at his own pace with very little classroom exposure. He had found his calling.

Once he realized what the result would be, what his life would be, there was no stopping that spirit who had once loved to learn and play with others. Bradley would never be locked away in a classroom or an office. He would be out in the world.

Joan, Bradley, and I all knew this was the best outcome we could have hoped for. Everything worked out for Bradley, and now Joan realized she hadn't failed him at all. He had everything under control, and she played her part perfectly. She had supported him and tried to help where she could. And now she knew and truly understood – it was his life to live, and he was going to be just fine.

CHAPTER 3:

PAST AND PRESENT CONNECTIONS

"Meow, meow."

Often when I'm at the gym I reach a lovely place of peace when I am jogging on the treadmill. Some people call it the zone. Amateurs and professional athletes strive to find this wonderful place because once you're there, you feel no pain, and everything is effortless. But for me it's different. For me, it opens a door or plane of existence. It lets all types of things come through.

"Meow, meow."

At the gym one day, while happily jogging in my zone, I saw a woman. She came to the gym regularly, and I heard other ladies call her Maureen. Today, in particular, she caught my attention. Maybe not her, but definitely what followed her around the exercise floor – two steps behind her trailed a big calico cat.

No one else paid any notice. Why would they? The cat that followed Maureen had passed from this world – it was a ghost.

"Meow, meow, just tell her I am here." The cat begged. "Please, I know she misses me and I have something I need her to know. Please, meow, please, meow, please, please, please, meow..."

Her cat would not leave me alone. She simply hung around getting under foot and meowing relentlessly. So I silently promised the cat if the opportunity presented itself, I would let her owner know *but* only if the opportunity came up.

It is quite common for pets to stick around after they die. Like people, many just want the living to know they are okay. But when they come to the gym, and get all snippy because you don't talk to their owner - that can be annoying.

I had finished my workout, and felt confident I had escaped a very awkward conversation. Wrong.

Most times I tune out ghosts and spirits. I don't say anything because it really freaks out the living. There is a time and place for everything, and the gym is neither. But what an insistent little creature! Tuning it out was not going to happen that day.

As I walked out of the change room, I ran smack dab into Maureen.

"Do you have a dead cat?" Okay, I wasn't that blunt. But how do you introduce something like this nicely?

I lowered my eyes, took a deep breath, and as tactfully as possible blurted out, "Did you have a calico cat that passed away recently?"

As usually happens, the poor lady just stood there open mouthed. I felt like an idiot. It's unbelievable how I get myself into these situations. But now that I started, I had to keep going – so I continued.

"Well, she is with you now and wants you to know everything is okay and that she still spends a lot of time with you. However, she is not comfortable coming to the gym. While she loves being with you, at the gym she is scared she might get her tail stepped on or caught in something. So from now on, she wants me to tell you, she will wait for you in the car."

Maureen looked at me with shock as tears welled up in her eyes.

"Oh, Tootsie ... she passed away last week. We always called her our little calico. Just last night I felt her jump on my bed, right beside me. I had to look twice before I remembered she was gone. And she always was paranoid about getting her tail stepped on or caught in something!"

A look of satisfaction crossed Maureen's face, "I knew I felt her. I told my husband, but he just made fun of me and called me silly, so I stopped saying anything – but I knew."

We are often thrown together with people. Is it just by accident, or is it part of some intricate plan? I never did believe in accidents.

As you can imagine, Maureen and I talked more after that bizarre introduction. She was a fascinating lady, and throughout her life she had many spiritual encounters. She rarely talked about these odd events because she did not understand them, and people often made fun of her when she tried. So I found my role was to help her understand. She was no longer alone. She had someone to discuss all this weird stuff with and learn how to tap into that side of herself.

But why? Why was I destined to meet and help Maureen? Trust me there have been many other times when I have successfully gotten out of a situation without blurting out, "I can see your dead cat." I wanted to understand why it was so important I have a friendship with Maureen in particular? I asked, and this is the story I was shown.

I saw myself as a young boy in a monastery in Siam. Every day the monks gathered us into groups for our lessons. We sat for several hours respectfully listening to the masters, and then we had chores to do. I spent most of my time in the gardens working with a very special man. Here my true learning took place, for Koshin was a very old and wise monk, skilled in the secrets of the old ways. He became my true master, teacher, and friend.

It was a difficult time for my master because the monarchy no longer approved of such primitive ways. In the garden, I learned about herbs and other substances that could be used to help people. Koshin secretly taught me practices to help the sick, to help those in childbirth, and ultimately to help ease those passing into the next world.

This monk was very knowledgeable and truly skilled in the old ways. Many people would have died if not for his ancient treatments.

Koshin loved to teach but knew that only a few could be trusted with this knowledge. If for any reason the king found out what he was teaching, Koshin would be killed in a very nasty public way. The monk's death would be an example to prove the old ways were outdated and would no longer be tolerated. The king was bringing in a new era.

As I continued to learn, I often accompanied Koshin out of the monetary. Another boy became extremely jealous of the time we spent together. Coincidentally, many times after we returned, the king summoned the monk to appear before him. The king demanded explanations for events that happened in the monastery and surrounding villages, especially those regarding miraculous healings.

Only a select few knew the particulars about these events. We began to suspect – a spy within our walls.

Thankfully, the king never got enough evidence to condemn Koshin or me. The people we helped would not admit to any wrong doings on the part of the monk, nor his student. They knew the treatments worked and that we were too valuable to lose.

One day the king's son became very ill. All the best doctors were sent for but to no avail. As his son grew worse, the king secretly sought out the monk – Koshin. "Cure my son, and you will live," the king commanded. "I will never again bring you before this court to answer for charges against you. Do whatever is necessary."

But the king had waited too long. The only thing that could be done was to help the boy pass more easily and quickly to the next life. However, by doing so, Koshin would expose his knowledge and be killed for not saving the boy. He would also expose his students, namely me, to the king's wrath as he would need supplies only the knowledgeable ones would be able to find.

Koshin took a risk and sent the monastery's top graduated student to do what he could for the king's son. He sent the jealous boy we suspected of being the king's spy.

The king's son went through a month of pain and suffering that were unnecessary. Since the graduate feared he would be put to death if the boy died, he tried everything to prolong the boy's life.

Surprisingly, when the relief of death finally came for the boy, the king sent the informant back to the monastery. The spy had specific instructions – to gather everything he could on Koshin. The monk would be destroyed, the king would see to it.

The old monk knew what ultimately would come to pass, so while the traitor was with the king, Koshin sent me away. He sent me to a remote village high in the mountains to tend their sick and create a life. I went as a healer not a monk.

I met a girl and we had four children. My eldest daughter, also had the gift to heal so I taught her what my master had taught me. I hoped by teaching her all the different herbs and practices of the old ways, the knowledge would be passed on to future generations.

Many years had passed when word came that Koshin had been executed for killing a high ranking official, who conveniently opposed the king. I knew the charges were all fabricated, but none-the-less, the king finally managed to get his revenge.

My mentor, my teacher, my friend, a person who meant so much to me in that life is Maureen in this one. No wonder this relationship had to be remembered.

But the story of Maureen and I did not end there. Siam was only the first life we shared. I needed to discover another piece of the puzzle to finally put the entire connection between Maureen and me together.

I entered the next life to find myself lying on a stretcher – dying. As I opened my eyes and looked around, I found myself in a filthy aid station just off the front line. The smell of death and mournful sounds of the dying were all around me. My pain seemed distant, but I knew I would not be here long.

Two doctors were in discussion a few feet away. One said, "You will try to save him! Do a leg amputation to stop the gangrene from spreading, remove the bullet from his chest and that's an order. Just think, if he dies, you can use it for your beloved research papers." They were discussing me.

When the younger doctor turned and I looked into his eyes, I knew. He was Maureen, my master, my teacher, and my friend. The doctor, who was his superior, was the jealous boy, the informant, the spy, who had ultimately caused Koshin's execution.

In this life, Maureen was tormented day after day for the decision Koshin made to send the informant to save the king's son. The monastery's top student had tried everything on the king's son, putting his patient through unnecessary pain and suffering for almost a month. The memories and knowledge of failure haunted the young monk for that entire life. His reputation was destroyed, and he spent the rest of his life as a servant and informant in the monastery.

This life seemed to be his time for revenge and he took it out on Maksim, the young Russian doctor under his command.

Many times, Maksim faced this exact, no win situation, and many times, it had ended in pain, suffering, and only finally with the sweet release of death. Not today.

Something happened when Maksim glanced into the eyes of that dying soldier – me. There was a connection. A peace settled over the doctor's tormented soul. The peace came in an instant as he realized the torture would not happen this time.

Never again would he give in. Never again would he carve up a dying soldier on his superior's sadistic command.

With that decision firmly held in his heart, the doctor came over to me, put his hand on my bloody chest and said, "Don't worry my old friend, everything will be okay."

Maksim spoke to a nurse and left.

Over the next several hours, that nurse came over many times to check on me and offer words of comfort. Maksim had given orders that nothing more was to be done. I was to die that day, but my passing was not to be prolonged in pain. I simply slipped quietly and peacefully into death.

I will never forget what Maksim did for me that day, and I guess I never did.

These two lives explained the connection Maureen and I shared. Once she helped me live and once she let me die. I owe her so much. And now, in this life is my chance to pay some of it back – to teach her and put her mind a peace, as she once did for me.

I don't know which was funnier – what I blurted out about her dead cat or what I blurted out next time I saw her, "You let me die! Thank you Maureen – for letting me die."

CHAPTER 4:

HOLDING IN A LONG FORGOTTEN SECRET

Colette had a problem, an extremely embarrassing problem that impacted her entire life. Every time she went out, she wondered if her affliction would strike.

When Colette arrived in my office, she was surprisingly comfortable with using hypnosis to find the cause. She wanted to put this issue in the past and be able to start a new, more freeing chapter of her life.

There were many demands for her to be in public settings as her career matured. When she received a new position, her business commitments increased substantially. There were daily meetings, and she attended networking functions on a regular basis.

She was constantly making excuses for not attending functions, and knew it had begun to hurt her professional success. It had gotten so bad she was now avoiding family gatherings as well. It had become too much.

She was ready to learn the truth – Why was she always constipated and hence so very gassy?

Clients come with a wide variety of symptoms. My role is to help them find the cause behind those symptoms, the story where it all began. When you find and understand the cause, the symptoms fade away. Every story is different. Even though the symptoms may be similar, no two stories are ever the same.

Being part of a large family and living in a house with only one bathroom presented many challenges for Colette as a young girl. She would just get into the bathroom and sit down, when her siblings would start knocking at the door. There were constant interruptions.

As she sat in my office, I watched her face transform into the frustrated pout of a small child. Her closed eyes focused on that distant door. When she finally relaxed and let herself flow with the memories, her subconscious whisked her back to another door when she was even younger.

"I remember this door very distinctly," she told me. "The doorknob was on the left, not like any of our previous doors. Somehow it felt backwards because when you stepped inside the bathroom, you ended up standing right in front of the bathtub."

That specific day the door was closed but unlocked, and as Colette rushed in, she interrupted her mother having a bath. Her mother modestly tried to cover herself. Even though Colette had more business to do, she quickly peed and left the bathroom.

"I was very young, I felt awkward and uncomfortable. I never told anyone," she said in a small voice.

While Colette sat in the chair across from me I watched her closely. Her relaxed hands had moved instinctively to cover her stomach.

Physical movements by people under hypnosis often provide insight to what their subconscious is trying to hold onto. If you address the feelings behind the movements, new information can be flushed out.

I pushed Colette's subconscious for more. "Colette, why are you holding your stomach? What are you feeling?"

Through a grimace she replied, "Suddenly I feel nauseated and very heavy, like I haven't gone to the bathroom and I desperately need to."

This was the first piece of the puzzle.

Colette did not understand why her subconscious would take her to such an embarrassing memory. Frustrated, she left that scene to discuss another. She insisted it was silly and had no relevance – but it did.

The subconscious often gives you hints, but your conscious steps in and tells you these details are unimportant. Take note of everything, even if it does not fit at the time.

The next door Colette found herself outside of was unfamiliar. It was old and wooden, and as Colette peeked inside, once again she was a child. How do I know, you might ask? Simple, even though her *adult* body sat on my office chaise, she reached up to grasp an invisible handle.

She found herself in a large white room with wooden floor. Once again the adult Colette spoke but this time with disappointment. "The room is empty. There is no furniture, but it definitely has a Victorian feel."

"Look around. What do you see?"

With eyes closed, in a full trance, Colette's head scanned my office as she scanned the Victorian house. "On my right appears to be a kitchen, and on my left is an open door to a bedroom."

Guided by her subconscious, Collette automatically headed for the bedroom. She began her description with an interesting discovery.

"The door is backwards. The handle is on the left. There is a large four-poster, canopy bed in the middle of the room with lace curtains and floral bedspread. On one side is a small child's vanity set and on the other, a woman's mirror and chest of drawers."

"Look in the mirror Colette, who do you see?" I told her.

"I am a small girl with dark brown hair. It curls around my shoulders as I brush it. I am still wearing my nightgown with small pink bows on it." Then she whispered, "And no one else is around – just me."

"Who lives here?" I inquired as if asking a forbidden secret. But Colette did not answer, she was too busy brushing her imaginary long hair.

I instructed Colette to leave the little girl's body so the girl could continue to brush her hair. We had other business.

"We are like detectives searching for clues, Colette. Where should we start? Remember what brought us here. How does this place relate to that issue? Where is the first clue?"

"The chest of drawers, top drawer," she said with conviction. As Colette opened the drawer to peek inside, she spoke in a sultry voice, "Woman's fancy underwear – garters and stockings, lacy corsets, and panties."

"Whose?"

"My mother's, of course."

"Sometimes people keep things hidden in their underwear drawer," I told her. "Is there anything else in there?"

Colette searched under the lace and looked surprised at what she found. "It's a woman's pearl handled knife." Switching to the girl's voice she added, "Yes, it's small and delicate but effective enough."

Apparently, the child was quite familiar with the knife.

"Why does she have it?"

"For protection," Colette said with a menacing sneer.

"Mother keeps it here, in our room, to protect us," the little girl said.

It is typical for individuals to switch between personalities while in a trance. One minute Colette had a scowl on her face as if remembering some hidden secret and the next she pretended to brush her hair.

My curiosity always piqued, Colette and I continued our search. "If you wanted to hide something else, Colette, where would it be?"

"In the closet." Colette confidently looked across the room.

"I see a beautiful green velvet dress with white trim – Mother wears that for fancy outings. I see a plain simple dress – Mother wore that one in the photo in the sitting room." Colette would find the items, but the little girl would tell us about them.

Fascinating. Colette's voice changed between the two characters, so we knew who was speaking – effortlessly completing each other's sentences.

Collette continued searching the room until something drew her attention. She instinctively stretched up trying to get it. On the top shelf, out of the little girl's prying reach, sat a hat box.

Colette knew there was no hat in that box. She pulled the ribbon to open the lid and found the box was filled with letters. They were addressed to Abigail, the mother, and simply signed, William.

"These are from her lover. She was cheating on my father. While my father was away fighting a war, my mother and this accountant were having an affair." These were Colette's words (or maybe an older version of the girl), and they were filled with anger and hurt.

As I glanced at the small girl quietly sitting, brushing her hair, I wondered – did she know?

And as quickly as I thought it, Colette answered, "She knows. She caught them once, here in this very bed. Mother tried to cover herself and lied to her daughter, saying the man was Uncle Bill."

Colette unconsciously held her stomach. When I asked how this new information made her feel, her response was oddly familiar. "I feel nauseated and very heavy".

Her mother told the child this was their secret. Uncle Bill had come to surprise their father, and she would be very upset if the little girl wrecked the surprise.

"Some things have to be held inside to protect the ones we love," the mother tried to explain. "Sometimes we have to put other's needs ahead of our own. It can be a hard burden to hold, but we hold it for the good of everyone. And if by chance it comes out, there will only be pain and embarrassment for you and hurt for those around you."

Several years later when the father returned home, tragedy struck. Her father was killed in that bedroom by an intruder. The intruder was allegedly looking for jewelry and had stabbed her father with a small but effective pearl-handled knife. Uncle Bill was there to help her mother pick up the pieces of her life and soon became the girl's step-father. The secret was buried deep inside that little girl, for now more than ever only pain and embarrassment would come from the release of that piece of information.

Seeing her mother naked had tripped a past life memory. A memory of holding something in for the benefit of the family and holding the belief that letting that secret out would result in pain and suffering. She also remembered the nauseated and very heavy feeling associated with keeping the secret in.

The puzzle pieces were falling into place.

However, Colette's visions suddenly stopped.

Most clients do not go into a past life so easily, nor retrieve such detailed information in their first session. Colette did. But evidently her subconscious' need to release its burden only went to a specific point. This was that point. Once again everything in Colette's system seized. She could not retrieve any more information. Her connection to the past life broke.

To get the rest of the story, I had to travel into Colette's past, and bring back the details we needed. If we wanted to uncover the meaning behind her physical condition, we needed to reveal the key information that was hidden with the secret. So, like in that lifetime, we had to unravel the mystery surrounding her father's death.

Colette and the other children were out playing, and her father was at work. Uncle Bill was *visiting* her mother.

On that fateful day, Father became ill and came home early. To his shock and horror, he caught his wife and trusted friend just as Colette had several years earlier – in a lover's embrace in his own bed.

A fight ensued. In an act of desperation, her mother reached into the drawer and pulled out that small pearl-handled knife. Without thinking, she plunged it into her husband's back. As her husband fell, he landed on the chair that sat in front of the little girl's vanity set. The chair splintered and impaled her father through the heart. He died instantly.

In a panic Bill and her mother made it look like a burglary and summoned the police. They got away with it. No one questioned the horrible scene or the grief stricken widow who was now faced with raising three young children on her own.

Bill came to the financial rescue several months later and married Colette's mother. However, her mother never recovered from the guilt.

Several years later, her mother took her own life. A suicide note revealed the horrible truth of what happened the day her husband died. Unfortunately, the truth only increased the pain and suffering of an already difficult situation.

In one mighty swoop, the family was destroyed. Bill went to prison for accessory to manslaughter. Her parents were both dead, and Colette and her siblings were sent to an orphanage.

Life for the children was not pleasant, but the worst was for Colette. Throughout that entire life, she blamed herself for not saying something sooner.

Maybe fate stepped in because she had not played her part. Maybe her father was supposed to find out and because she didn't tell him, he had to see for himself. Maybe if she had revealed the secret, her father would be alive. Maybe both her parents would be alive. And maybe they would still be a happy family.

So what was the moral of the story? What was Colette supposed to learn? As we went through the particulars of that life,

Colette realized the similarities to her current one. The main similarity between the two was – keeping secrets.

Colette realized how often she kept secrets, withholding information in the attempt to prevent hurt feelings or unpleasant consequences. In her childhood Colette learned little white lies were acceptable, even preferable to provoking grand displays of emotions. These white lies expanded as she grew older. Her family members began keeping bigger and bigger secrets from one another. Even at work, lies were part of the corporate game. Things were no longer right or wrong. The truth lay somewhere between. Secrets had become a big part of her life.

When Colette thought back, she discovered that keeping secrets and little lies never ended well. The truth always came out, ironically at the most inopportune times, and caused her a lot of distress. Usually more distress than if the information would have come out in the beginning. Keeping secrets *in* caused her more issues in *the end*.

Colette's conscious, subconscious, and body were very good at holding things in. But, the less she spoke about awkward information or emotions, the more physical pain she had to endure. Eventually her constipation, nausea, and heaviness got so bad, her health dictated what she could do in her life.

Colette needed to work on the lesson of letting go, literally and figuratively.

Regret, living in the past, and the what-ifs, kept Colette bound up. In addition, she had to remember all the particulars of each lie so she wouldn't get caught. All this had Colette's guts constantly in knots.

Her health issues and subconscious finally pushed her to expose past secrets. Secrets that had her living in a spiritual loop. By exploring those events she got unstuck and discovered several lessons she was supposed to work on.

One can only do what they believe to be right at the time. If one decides to hold on to information, they can't look back and be mad at doing so. They have to let that decision go. The past can't be changed. Learn from it and move forward.

Souls create things to happen in their lives. They create situations to help them learn. No one is responsible for screwing up another soul's life or journey. It's all part of the plan. Remember the context. We are looking at the *soul's* journey and that journey transcends individual lives.

CHAPTER 5:

SCREAMS IN THE NIGHT

I opened the door to greet my new client when a tremendous cold came over me. But only when she mentioned going on an Alaskan cruise, did I realize why. In that moment, just like that, I found myself standing on the deck of sailing ship.

Icebergs surrounded me. I shivered at the sheer size of them – large and majestic. As the sun came over the horizon, the icebergs shone with a ghostly green glow – like something alien reaching up from beneath.

In the stillness of the morning, unearthly sounds touched my body and soul. As the ice cracked and shifted – it created a mournful cry, making the hair on the back of my neck, stand up and a chill lodge in my heart. The place took on an eerie quality. Pieces of ice fell away and sank into the sea lost from view, as if calling to me, warning me.

I had tripped into one of Carol's past lives.

Carol had come to me for Reiki. She was in her seventies, and the winter weather always took its toll on her joints. As the snow began to fly, her legs would ache, but her real pain began as the ice formed on the river. Just like the ice, pain would move over her body until she could scarcely move. She would remain that way – frozen, until the spring thaw.

Reiki is another tool I use in my practice. It involves working with energy of the physical, mental, emotional, and spiritual bodies. For me, Reiki opens not just the Chakras, but an information path to the other side.

When we worked on her physical body, other pains within her came to light. Several years before, Carol placed her husband in a long term care facility. The decision had not been an easy one.

I am quite familiar with the reality of not being able to care for the elderly. My mother is a nurse in a long term care facility and I have many clients, family, and friends who have found themselves in similar circumstances. Carol did not have the same perspective. As she put it, "I locked him away in an institution until he died." Her guilt and pain were obvious.

Her husband had Alzheimer's and it had become too hard for her to look after him at home. Carol wanted a place where they would properly take care of him. She hadn't just put her husband in the first facility she looked at. She searched until she found him a place that kept high standards.

The facility where he stayed was very clean and had security measures so her husband could not wonder off as he tended to do at home. The walls, ceiling, and floor were all white, so it would be easy to see if things needed to be cleaned or hadn't been. It had a nice pleasant smell, like the outdoors, not the antiseptic smell many other facilities had. The staff wore uniforms, and the ward was locked. She knew her husband would be healthy and safe. Unfortunately, that did not mean he would be happy.

He hated it. He did not understand way she had dumped him there and just left. The food was always cold and they kept the temperature way too low. He was always freezing. Carol tried to explain that he was cold because of his diabetic medicine, but he would always forget by the next visit. To him it was simple. He begged her to take him home.

It was sad to hear that even after his death Carol still lived with the nightmare of seeing his pleading smile in the window as she drove away. "He never understood," she said. "He just never understood."

We didn't discuss the guilt she lived with because, frankly, Carol didn't want to.

I tell people all the time, lessons are stored like boxes on a shelf. Your subconscious brings them down for you to work on, but it's your choice if you open the box. If you choose not to, don't worry, the boxes will still be there – this lifetime or the next. Eventually you will have to open them all. This comment usually inspires begrudging consent to at least look at the box, if not open it.

Not Carol. Carol dealt with the box by putting it back on the shelf. She just wanted to focus on the future. She was going on vacation, one she had dreamt of all her life – she was going on an Alaskan cruise.

I knew she had been there before, just not in this life and not as a woman.

In the 15th and early 16th centuries, Europe needed to find a faster trade route to bring riches from Asia. People would pay handsomely for these luxuries. Many ships were sent exploring and many lives lost in the pursuit.

Two brothers decided to tempt fate and make their fortunes on the high seas.

They would scrape together all the money they had, plus the pay they received from working on board ship, to buy goods in China. The goods would then be taken back home to sell. They discussed cotton or tea but determined silk would probably be the easiest to transport. It did not matter what they brought back, they would be rich. It would be a grand adventure.

One morning, well into their journey, they woke to good weather. Blue and white as far as you could see. The snow-covered land stretched out to join the glacier ice flow. Where one stopped and the other began you couldn't tell. The blue of the sea meld seamlessly into the sky, marred only be the reflected sun. It was mesmerizing.

Maurice and Rene volunteered to go ashore to get fresh water and hopefully find some fresh meat. There were minor repairs to be done on the ship, but hunting was a lot more fun, so the boys jumped at the chance to go.

They ventured over the ridge to see what they could find. Repairs should not take long and they had to be back by early afternoon. They promised not to go too far from the ship, just over the first ridge.

The weather was getting colder, but the boys were happy to be on solid ground. The wind was picking up, and they couldn't see their tracks behind them. Trying diligently to keep his bearings, Maurice constantly fell behind as he stopped to check of the ship's location on the horizon. They would freeze to death if they couldn't get back to the ship.

Maurice followed Rene as they climbed the ridge and began to descend the other side. The grandeur of the scene was incredible – nothing but open space, not even a single tree, only white and more white. It was like God had waved his mighty hand and cleared everything. It was untouched and serene. A calm hovered over them – like the peace before a storm – and then, in a breath, the earth opened up, and Maurice was gone.

Rene looked back just in time to see his brother disappear. As he ran back up the slope, Rene prayed it was just a trick of the northern light. Like always, his brother would be there waiting, and he would tease Rene for panicking over nothing.

Not this time.

Maurice was wedged in a crevasse, just wide enough for him to slip in and get himself stuck. He looked up at his brother with a pleading smile and told him to get help. Rene did not want to leave.

He laid face down and tried to anchor his feet in the snow, but couldn't reach. He flipped around, putting his feet down the hole. He hoped using his hands would give him better grip to get a little further – a little closer, within reach. He kept trying to reach his brother, he knew, if he stretched a bit more, he could get him out.

Maurice knew the more Rene tried, the weaker the edge of the crevasse became. If the edge gave way, they would both be trapped with no hope of rescue. Rene had to go.

There were no goodbyes.

Rene promised he would return soon with more men and get Maurice out. As fast as he could, Rene ran up over the ridge and back to the ship.

The crew knew something was wrong. For as long as they had known them, the brothers were always together. When they heard what had happened, they collected ropes and a board to use as a sled to get Maurice back to the ship. Bad weather was moving in quickly, but they would not leave without Maurice.

They came to the top of the ridge and were struck by the barren, snow-covered landscape – everything looked the same. There were no landmarks nor any trace of where Maurice had fallen through the snow.

The crew spent hours searching, calling out to Maurice, but to no avail. The wind was now howling so loud they could have been mere steps away and probably not been able to hear him call – that is, if he was still able to call. Everyone knew how quickly a man could freeze out there, and if he had been injured in the fall – Maurice might already be dead.

There was nothing they could do. Night had fallen and silence had fallen over the group. If he was not dead now, he would be by the time they could resume the search the next morning. The captain had no choice. He would not risk the remaining crew. It was over. It was time to leave.

They held a small ceremony for Maurice and travelled on. The crew never spoke of leaving him behind. They never voiced their agonizing fear – of sailing away, leaving Maurice trapped alive, alone to die. They all hoped he died quickly, maybe even before Rene had got back to the ship. It was a tragic accident.

Rene was never the same. Every night after, for the entire voyage, he would awake to his own screams. He would find himself lying in a pool of freezing sweat with the haunting memory of those desperate eyes looking up at him and that smile that pleaded, "Come back for me. You have to come back."

The captain sent news of the tragedy back to Maurice's family. Rene changed ships and sailed for several more seasons. But eventually it was time to go home. Rene never knew exactly what the captain had written, but he always felt his family blamed him for his brother's death. And why not, he also felt it *was* his fault.

Rene never forgave himself. He should have marked the spot so they could have found Maurice. Maybe if they had helped with the repairs and not volunteered to go hunting. Maybe if he had stayed closer to his brother. Even if they both had fallen, at least, they would have died together. Maybe, just maybe. Anything would have been better than this.

I snapped back to our session and gently relayed the story to Carol. She looked at me and declared, "I did it again. I left my husband trapped and afraid, to die alone, and it was all my fault."

How did she get it so wrong? "No," I said, "you were Maurice. Your husband was Rene."

Everything slipped into place. Maurice spent his last hours blaming Rene. "How could he?" Rene spent a lifetime with the guilt, blaming himself. "How could I?" Never forgiving and never seeing the other side.

Well, they got to see the other side in this life, and surprisingly, in many other lives as well.

Carol spent a decade in Rene's shoes. She was forced, by circumstance, to lock her beloved husband away. Ironically, she put him in a very similar environment to where Maurice had once been trapped: white walls, cold, constantly waiting – feeling betrayed. No wonder she was haunted, remembering those desperate eyes looking out at her and that pleading smile that said, "Come back for me. You have to come back."

Even before her husband passed away, Carol had to endure the guilt and blame of locking him away in an institution. His family did not understand. Unless you had experience with someone who had Alzheimer's, you couldn't understand. One minute they are fine and the next they do not know who you are. They, themselves, do not understand. They don't feel sick. They often feel betrayed and alone.

As the truth of the situation began to sink in, Carol did not want to talk about it. Back on the shelf went the box. She went on her cruise, and I was surprised she came to see me when she got back.

"How was your cruise?" I asked. "Was Alaska as beautiful as people say?" I tried to keep the topic light and fluffy.

Tears welled up in her eyes as she told me she was sick in her stateroom the entire trip. All the emotions were bottled up inside her, and she wanted it over. She knew she had to deal with what had happened in this life and in the past.

So she asked, "How do I let it go?"

Carol had to learn to forgive so she could get past the story and see the lessons hidden within. First she had to forgive Rene for leaving her in that snowy tomb and then she had to forgive herself for putting him in an institution. After all this, she could see that sometimes there really is no choice. Just as in this life she had no choice but to place her husband, in *that* life Rene had no choice but to leave his brother. It was something neither of them wanted to do, and they fought against it as long as they could, but in the end they had to leave their loved one and go on. But going on did not mean they forgot. Nor did it mean they were happy with the choice they were forced to make.

Once Carol let go of the anger, guilt, and grief of these two events, we moved on and began looking for the lesson she was supposed to learn.

Collecting all the bits of information we had gathered, we realized an important piece of the puzzle had come up months before.

We didn't know where it fit — until now — and even now it took some work for it to fall into place.

There was a pattern between her two lives, but also within Carol's current life. Almost thirty years ago, Carol had a daughter, who died at 23 in a bizarre traffic accident. She was in the wrong place at the wrong time, and in an instant she was gone. Carol always blamed the driver of the vehicle involved and never addressed her own feelings of anger, guilt, or grief at the loss of her daughter. Again, it was a similar story — the question was, what was Carol suppose to learn from it?

Every soul comes to the physical plane to learn things. Everyone has their own agenda and plan. Their own journey. When people come in and out of our lives, it is to help us learn and to help them learn. When someone dies, we are not supposed to stop living; we are supposed to continue on and learn.

Some say we die when we have learned all our lessons for that life. Others say dying is to help someone else learn a lesson. Either way, wallowing in despair does not help anyone learn nor does pushing the pain so deep within us that we lose its meaning. Like a toothache, living with pain does not help nor does ignoring it — it just leads to a bigger mess in the end.

There are many lessons imbedded in these stories, but I believe the paramount one that Carol needed to see was that emotions are part of the learning and part of the journey. We are here in physical form to experience emotions, and we can't just bury them when they are unpleasant.

When emotions are buried, they fester and can create physical issues in the body. Carol never realized that holding all that hurt and pain inside was not just preventing spiritual growth but also causing many of her physical ailments.

Things like anger, blame, and guilt do not change the reality of the facts, but they do indicate things about us that we need to investigate. Why we are feeling these emotions has a lesson within it. Emotions help and guide us to the lessons we have set out to learn. Therefore when these emotions are ignored, situations evolve or escalate until we are forced to stop and reflect.

Carol's health issues could be traced back to corresponding emotional times in her life. During our sessions, any time big emotional issues came up, Carol did not want to talk about them. Until finally, the connection was made, and she realized not dealing with her emotions was literally making her sick.

I find dealing with emotions leads to issues and dealing with issues releases something deep inside us. It is like a cleanse. Like Barb described it in a previous story, it feels like a giant weight finally being lifted.

As we went through this process, Carol's physical ailments got noticeable better, and the following winter she was planning another trip to Alaska. This time she would honor that previous life, and with the release of her anger and guilt, she knew she would have a spectacular journey.

CHAPTER 6:

STUCK IN THE DETAILS

Dwayne had a strange compulsion – he collected cattle.

Now when I say he collected cattle, that's literally what he did. Dwayne would go to auctions and buy cattle. With every cent he had, he would buy cattle. Even when he had to borrow money, if the cow or bull looked good, he had to have it.

The problem with collecting live animals is, they're alive. You can't just put them on a shelf and admire them. You have to be *involved*. Cattle need to be cared for – fed, watered, sheltered – little things that keep them living. Dwayne didn't seem to understand.

Some people want cattle to breed – not Dwayne.

Other people want cattle for dairy stock – not Dwayne.

Perhaps to slaughter and eat, or store for later – not Dwayne.

Maybe as a pet? No, not Dwayne.

What else could it be?

His only focus was having them. What happened after he bought them was of no concern.

On several occasions, Dwayne found himself in legal trouble over neglecting his cattle. Many times his mother and aunt helped him, both physically and financially – from early morning drives to feed the cows and help during calving, to paying fines and creditors. But they had had enough. Something had to change.

Kerri was Dwayne's aunt but also my client. And when she arrived for her session, I could tell she was distracted. She came, sat down, and without any how-do-you-do, went right into her dilemma.

Originally, Kerri sought out a hypnotherapist for weight loss. But when strange conversations like this come up, I respectfully followed what I call the bouncing ball. When trying to find the cause behind issues, I knew – important information hides in weird places. Obviously it was of great concern to her, and I must say, it had my curiosity piqued. Remember, always follow the bouncing ball.

"Did you ever talk to him about it?" I asked.

"Oh yeah," she said. "Last weekend he bought another bull on credit. My sister was livid, so I asked Dwayne why he did it. He simply looked down at his empty hands in silence."

Both Kerri and Dwayne were brought up on farms. Kerri could understand buying a cow, having it butchered, and packing it away in the freezer but she couldn't understand her silent nephew.

She went on. "Then do you know what he said?"

I shook my head, anxiously awaiting the answer.

"He sheepishly confessed he had no clue why he did it." Kerri sarcastically wiggled her fingers in the air saying, "Something comes over him and he's just gotta have them – just in case."

She laughed in frustration, "Just in case. Just in case of what?"

That was the question, and that was the story I was determined to find.

After we completed Kerri session, she left and I went searching for some answers. I put myself in a trance and connected to one of Dwayne's past lives.

In a little shack, in the middle of nowhere, lived a family. A young man of twenty-two managed to save enough money to buy a small parcel of land. He had worked for others – cutting lumber, clearing land, even working on the railroad – but now it was time to settle down. This young man was Dwayne.

He took his new bride to this middle of nowhere. They built a temporary shelter while he cleared land for a house. It was backbreaking work, but Dwayne and his wife were happy.

They put in a garden and made do with what game he could hunt. Things would get better when they cleared enough land for their house and crops. But their situation started to change rather fast. Not even nine months later their first child was born, a healthy baby girl. Now there was another mouth to feed and for a while, one less pair of hands to help with the work.

That first winter was rough, and unfortunately it did not get any better. They put their house on hold to clear more land. By the end of summer they managed to plant potatoes and some corn to keep them through that winter. However, their goal of clearing enough land for a cash crop did not happen. There were too many trees and rocks. The extra money from a crop would have to wait at least another year.

Thank heavens, they got to know some of their neighbours over the winter so got some truly needed help that spring. Slowly they would learn what was best to plant, how to rotate crops, and how to store more food. That always seemed to be the priority – how to survive the winters.

The following year brought both sorrow and joy. Dwayne's wife had a stillbirth when their next child came too early, but after a bountiful spring, she gave birth to twins. Every year the family seemed to get a little ahead but were thrown back with another mouth or two to feed.

Their dream house was always on hold, but they expanded their small shelter. When the house became too small for the new baby, they would connect a granary or storage shed to the shack as an extra bedroom. And each bed could hold three or four children, so they made room for everyone. The cooking area was in the middle, and the bedrooms all connected to it. It was simple but very functional. Times were hard but slowly getting better.

Just as the family was finally pulling ahead, the drought came. The family had learned what to plant, how to store it, and where to hunt. But with no water during the summer, the seeds did not grow, there were no fruits or berries in the woods, nothing to store, and even the wildlife was dwindling. Times had gone from hard to impossible.

By this time, Dwayne and his wife had ten children from newborn to thirteen. As things got worse, he helplessly watched the little ones starve and his wife grow frail with despair. He sent the four oldest to town hoping they could find work, but they might have been better off withering away with the rest of the family. Town was no place for young, pretty girls in those days. They did what they had to do to survive.

During the next three years this young man lost everything and as he buried his wife beside six of his children, he reflected on what he could have done differently.

If only he had bought cattle. His family would have been so much better off when things went bad. Some of his neighbours had just a few, and it made all the difference. All he had needed was a few cows to sustain his family, but instead he had put everything into his crops.

Shortly after, Dwayne left his land and went to the big city. He was all alone once again. Eventually the government started helping the poor – providing aide and creating jobs. Dwayne worked in a soup kitchen and over the years helped feed the poor.

There was always sadness in his eyes, a distant but never forgotten pain. No matter how many people he helped feed, it couldn't change the past.

When war broke out in Europe, it was surprising how things got better in America. Factories were opened, and many women worked full time as the men were off fighting. But Dwayne continued to work with the poor, continued to give everything he could to their cause.

When he passed away, many people spoke of how generous he was with his time and what little money he had. And as I watched Dwayne's spirit leave that body, I heard his biggest regret – "Next time I will keep cattle, just in case."

Now things were starting to make sense. An interesting thing about past lives is that many times the spirit incorporates old scenarios into a new time period. Even though the setting has changed, often the story is the same even down to small, obscure details.

Perhaps we feel more comfortable learning our lessons in familiar settings. Perhaps the spirit just wants to set the stage with some familiar things so it does not have to start from scratch each time. It sets things up different enough in hopes of create happier outcomes, but still interweaves some recognizable details.

When Kerri came for another session, I shared the past life I visited and the insight I retrieved.

I explained how some people, in their current life, buy and store tremendous amounts of food because they died of starvation in a past life. Other people can be overweight because they starved during another life and want to ensure it won't happen again by physically storing extra weight. But this was the first time I had heard of a person collecting cattle to prevent starvation because they thought that was the solution in a previous life.

Kerri commented as she left that she and her older sister always stored food. They both had huge pantries full of dried and canned goods and freezers too – they always had, just like their mother. Storing food made sense to them, but they never understood Dwayne until today.

I gave one last piece of the puzzle to Kerri. We tend to go through lives with many of the same people just in different roles, I told her. We add some different characters here and there and sometimes we just give them more or less of a role. Some are background characters compared to our main co-stars.

In response to that slightly out of place comment she asked, "We were there too, weren't we?"

She had gotten my point. "Yes," I replied. "You and your sister were the twins."

A couple months later I heard from Kerri again. We had not seen each other since talking about Dwayne, but there were big changes in her life. Kerri had left our session and went straight to her sister's farm. She told her sister about Dwayne's past life. The story of starvation and how they swore to plan better the next time around. Later, her sister told Dwayne. (I wonder how she brought that into a conversation.)

That story made the difference. That story prompted the *change*. Because after that, Kerri lost thirty pounds, her sister lost forty-five pounds, and Dwayne started selling off some of his cattle.

I mentioned that familiarity can promote learning. But sometimes familiarity brings up behaviours that over-shadow learning, and we become compulsive about not ending up the same way. Sometimes the spirit has to be reminded that we live in a new age, a new time and in a new story.

In this life Kerri was a social worker who helped special needs adults learn how to become more self-sufficient so they can work and put food on their own tables. Her sister had a farm and at a young age married a rancher so they had a crop farm combined with a cattle ranch. And surprisingly, when they divorced and her husband took the cattle ranch, their son Dwayne left home and shortly after began his collection of cattle.

Everything was there – the patterns, the promises – still silently running in the background of the subconscious. By realizing this was a new time and different situation, they realized they didn't need quite as much or exactly the same things as they did in that past life. And with that realization they broke the cycle.

Hopefully by remembering the past, they will be able to move on with the other lessons they are here to learn instead of being stuck in the details.

CHAPTER 7:

SOMETIMES THINGS ARE NOT WHAT THEY APPEAR

"I would have been Attila the Hun." I overheard someone say.

We were at a company Christmas party and the stud of the group had somehow stumbled into my area of expertise.

With a drink in one hand and his other arm wrapped seductively around his wife, he puffed out his chest. "Well, isn't it obvious? We are so much alike. Attila was big and strong. He controlled an army of fighting men and was brilliant – and maybe a bit ruthless. That's who I would have been."

I'm not sure what the others thought, but when my husband turned to me, my face was burning. I faked a small cough. I try really hard not to laugh, but sometimes it is difficult – if they only knew.

Right before my eyes, this large, masculine construction worker began to transform.

His hair grew long and dark, and matched his feminine eyelashes. His shoulders and waist narrowed to a petite figure, while his hands became delicate and smooth. An almost transparent veil appeared across his face in a warm peach color. The veil was covered in tiny bells and matched the harem girl outfit that so perfectly displayed every curve.

A number of pastel layers slowly draped themselves atop the revealing costume nearly completing the transformation. The only thing that remained was his annoying voice chattering in the background. How could that low masculine voice be coming from this delicate beauty?

"I would crush my enemies with my bare hands." He just would not stop.

Jingle, jingle – wiggle, wiggle. With every word he spoke, the woman he had become danced. I could still see *his* bratty eyes in *her* pretty face, playfully teasing over the veil. She moved her hips with the most seductive emphasis and with every word, every wiggle, I heard bells. And worst, the more he talked – the more veils she would peel away and drop.

The tears were already starting. I had to excuse myself before I choked on my laughter.

Sometimes, all it takes is a few words, and visions start flashing before my eyes.

As curious as I am though, and as easy as it is to do, I don't snoop in other people's affairs unless I am asked. And even then, I have worked with the subconscious enough to know, your soul knows exactly what I am doing. If you do not want me to see something, your soul will stop me from poking around.

With that said, sometimes the pictures just come, as in the incident above.

Information is constantly flowing around everyone, and people like me can read it. For this reason, many individuals sensitive to this information isolate themselves and avoid large groups of people. They get overwhelmed. Fortunately, I have learned to shut it off. I just turn it off, like a light switch, and most of the times it works.

If the light switch *doesn't* turn off, I keep my mouth shut. I respect that we are all on journeys, and each of us needs to learn our own lessons. But I have come to the realization – sometimes people write me into their journeys. When people get stuck, they find me to get them unstuck.

So I have set up a rule: when I get unrequested information, whether for a client or someone in their lives – I will not say anything unless the opportunity arises.

If I am *not* supposed to tell them something, the conversation naturally takes a turn away from the information I have received. If I were to mention it at that point, it would feel out of place, so I leave it be. Maybe they are not ready to hear it yet or maybe it will complicate the lesson they are currently working on. Regardless, I keep it to myself unless it comes up in another conversation.

I leave everything to timing, and trust I will tell them the information when they are ready to hear it.

Rebecca, a client, brought one such story with her. This story insisted on being heard even though it involved her husband and not Rebecca herself. But irregardless, *her* subconscious had had enough of his story influencing their lives. She needed to understand the history of her husband's obsession to finally let go of her annoyance and frustration. If she let the issue fester much longer it would threaten their relationship.

"James has a real job, but that's not what brings us out West," Rebecca absently stated at the end of one of her sessions. The comment felt out of place so, for me, it instantly drew my attention.

I always assumed Rebecca had come West with her husband when he was here on business, but I was about to find out the sordid truth. A secret they had kept from most of their family – James had an obsession to find gold.

In his youth, James bought mineral rights on several parcels of land in northern British Columbia. As part of the deal, he had to come on a regular basis to work the claim – which for us laypeople means – pan for gold.

I didn't realize people still did that. Just like the demonstration at Fort Steele, you take a pan, a bit of dirt, and water from a stream, and then slowly swirl it until hopefully, you find tiny bits of gold sunk to the bottom. It is hard for me to imagine people nowadays having that much patience.

"When the kids were young, we used to go camping and have grand adventures while James panned for gold." A smile flickered across Rebecca's face, quickly replaced by an irritated scowl. "Looking back, I don't even know if he enjoyed it. He never talks about getting rich. It seems like work, more of an obligation than a passion."

And then it came – that familiar statement I hear so often.

"He tells me it's just something he has to do."

There it was again, the bait that always draws me in – like a taunt from a new puzzle, challenging me to solve it.

Of course her story hit a chord, but that last remark was what had left me pondering why? Why would a man go through all that trouble if he didn't enjoy it? And why spend all that time and money, for years, doing something when he didn't have a clue why? There must be a reason.

This time, before images started popping into my mind, the smell almost knocked me over. Rancid fish, stinky bodies, and salt. Oh, what a lovely combination!

Usually I am just thrown straight into a scene but once in a while when the smell or taste of something is significant, I get that sensation first. Unfortunately, so far, it's never been pleasant. Very effective at getting my attention, but never pleasant.

In the midst of the horrible stench, I found myself on the deck of a large ship. Sailors ran around in what appeared to be utter chaos. Some were in the rigging while others pulled ropes attached to the sails. Men yelled orders while others bellowed back responses. They lined the railings and each held some sort of weapon.

All of a sudden, everyone stopped and stood still ready to fight.

Curious, I looked up to see which flag the ship flew under. What country would claim such an unsavory group? As if on cue the main sail blew aside, and behind it, with a snap of wind, a most foreboding, yet strangely familiar flag unfurled. It was dark black and as ill-kempt as the crew itself. In the center of the black shone a white skull with bones beneath. The Jolly Roger? Not quite but it was similar enough that I knew – I was either on a pirate ship or a privateer. Either way, with this crew and that flag, things were about to get violent.

As the ship approached another, words were exchanged between the men on the upper decks. A young boy pulled down the black flag and hoisted a red one. Was it over? Thank goodness.

But no, I was wrong. It had just begun. Later I learned a red flag meant they intended to fight and would give no quarter, no mercy for the other side. And fight they did. When the smoke cleared and the dead lay sprawled about both ships, I discovered the man I knew to be Rebecca's husband. James had survived.

He was a big man, so it did not surprise me to see him alive. There would be a few more scars added to his collection, but he was okay. One thing that *did* surprise me, however, was that this experience was nothing like Johnny Depp's version of *Pirates of the Caribbean*. The smell alone could make you sick. The original smell of fish, salt, and sweat, was nothing compared to the stench of fear, gunpowder, and death that now hung over the ship. I knew I would have to shower later to get the awful smell out of my nose and my hair.

James belonged to a crew of British privateers. The captain had papers that allowed his ship to loot any Spanish ship they came across. Most of the booty they pillaged consisted of tobacco, sugar, rum, weapons, gunpowder, and ammunitions – but what they truly wanted was gold. Gold was the easiest thing to trade and divide among the crew.

While the captain had some distant ties and loyalty to the British Navy, James was entirely driven by his pursuit of gold. And the greater his desire, the more the gold seemed to elude him just like the rum slipped through his lips.

That's all I got, not how he died or how he lived. But I do know that he never satisfied his desire for gold. I can still hear him say, "Next time. I will find it next time."

Every time Rebecca came to see me, it tripped more of James' story.

It was cold, oh so cold. The wind was from the east, but the water's what truly made it cold. As he rummaged in the mountain stream, his fingers soon became numb. He tried to keep his boots dry, but he knew it wouldn't be long before his feet felt the same as his hands. The rest of the day would be spent with clumsy movements, for even when the air warmed up, the water was still mountain fed and freezing.

James had seen it happen to too many men before. Their fingers and toes turned black, and eventually...he was not going to think about it. When James stopped for the night, he always rubbed his feet and soaked them in hot water. His mother had taught him well, and after seeing that first case for himself, he always remembered.

James had a job to do, and nothing was going to get in his way. He had spent several years in California before a man named Louis told him about Dawson City. The real gold was to be found in the Yukon on the Klondike and Yukon Rivers. They pooled their resources and went north together. Even though he missed the warm weather in California, the Klondike was the place to be if he was serious about finding gold.

Like many who dreamed of gold, James and Louis were unprepared for the harsh conditions of the Klondike. The permafrost kept the ground hard. The glaciers kept the water ice cold. The endless searching kept the prospectors desperate, as desperate as the wolves that howled all night long. The money it took to get there and the cost of living in the area were exorbitant, so what little the men found went straight back into food and supplies.

This vision didn't last long either, but once again I was left with James' voice echoing in my ears, "Next time. I will find it next time." I only got a part of this life even less than the last. I don't

THE PORTAL TO PAST LIFE INSIGHT

know if he lived through the Gold Rush or died pursuing his gold. All I know was his search continued.

Sometimes you need a couple of lives to see the whole picture. I never asked to see James' story, but I kept getting glimpses of his pursuit. So when I sat down to write a new chapter for this book, and James' story insisted on being included – I didn't know how to finish it. All I had were bits and pieces with an underlying story about his search for gold. But every time I tried to write a different story, his would intervene. I knew James' had to be finished.

Actually, when looking for the end, I realized I didn't have the beginning either. Where did the story start? What was the cause of his constant desire to find gold? Once I asked the correct question, the answers flooded in.

The first thing I saw was a Spanish conquistador helmet. Then everything went black.

In the dark of the night a small pool of lamplight slowly illuminated the scene. James was driving a horse-drawn covered wagon and secretly meeting a Spanish officer named Don Francisco. Don Francisco looked after a port in the New World and ensured the Spanish king's interests. James was meeting the Don to pick up important cargo for his return trip back to Spain. Their meeting was clandestine.

When Don Francisco opened the chest he was delivering, James saw lots of different gold coins and artifacts. One figure stood out among the rest. At the top of the chest was an obsidian black jaguar with gold accents. It was almost a foot long and looked majestic as it sat on the pile of gold – protecting the gold for one of the Aztec gods. It had a haunting stare.

The Don closed and locked the chest, giving James the key. James loaded his precious cargo into the back of the wagon and left for the docks. All the precautions were taken with this treasure, for it now belonged to the King of Spain, and it was vital to the success of Spain's naval fleet.

63

The voyage home was long but happily uneventful. James was a good captain for the Vera Cruz, a ship the king had personally honored him with two years before.

When the Vera Cruz arrived in Spain, James personally took the chest to present to the king. He took the key from a chain around his neck and opened the chest. Everyone was astonished at what they saw – there was no gold in the chest only stones and rocks.

Rumors flew, and James was accused of treason. The usual punishment was death. But the king trusted James and remembered his genuine look of surprise as he threw open the lid of the chest. James was put in irons, and instead of being executed, he was ordered to the New World. There he would be a prisoner – to the one man James could assume must be responsible for the crime. Don Francisco, the man who had given him the chest and the key.

Francisco was the only one there that night. It had to be him who switched the chests. The king knew James would find a way to expose the true traitor. The king sent James on the Vera Cruz with his old crew, knowing some of them, if not all, would help him discover the truth.

When the Vera Cruz arrived in the New World, Don Francisco was notified that James had died in a storm at sea. However, James was hidden, and taken ashore secretly, to clear his name.

James asked many questions of the locals about the treasure and the beautiful obsidian jaguar. There were many myths about the black jaguar. And rumors about the treasure only perpetuated the myths. It was said that the jaguar was a servant of the Aztec gods and that it protected all Aztec gold. It was rumored that the jaguar used its mystical powers to steal the treasure from the locked chest during the transfer from Francisco to the ship. The jaguar returned the treasure to Quetzalcoatl, god of creation, giver of life, who was associated with self reflection.

As James' search continued, he discovered that Don Francisco had done nothing out of the ordinary after the chest was delivered that night. He had not changed in duty or station. He lived in the same house and performed routine tasks as always. As a result, it was difficult for James to conclude that Francisco had profited by stealing the treasure. The Don was well liked and respected, and as James got to know his character, he had to admit to himself that Don Francisco was not the thief.

Several other shipments of gold had been sent to Spain after James left the New World, and they all arrived at their destination without incident. It appeared the one shipment with the golden obsidian jaguar was destined to remain a mystery.

James spent the rest of that life trying to redeem his honor. He searched for gold throughout the area, sending whatever he found to the Don to be sent back to Spain. But James knew it was too little, and could not replace the lost shipment. He lived the rest of his life knowing his name would never be cleared. James died, labeled a traitor to his country and king.

I kept asking myself, "What lesson is to be learned? Is it simply that James is still trying to replace the lost gold to clear his name?" Then the last pieces of the puzzle fell into place.

When James was a privateer, he had been known for his honor among thieves. Many times when bloodlust struck the crew and they wanted to slaughter everyone on the captured ships, James would not let them. He was big enough that no one got between him and those he tried to protect. His captain was often inconvenienced by bringing captives to shore. But the captain was motivated by distant ties and loyalty to the British Navy, so slaughtering innocent sailors on trading ships was not his main goal. His main goal was keeping the supplies out of Britain's enemies' hands.

When James was in the Klondike, he had been known for his protection of women and children. Many times in the saloons and stores of Dawson City he stopped self-entitled miners from taking what was not offered. James again was big, and not many chose to get between him and those he tried to protect.

In this life, James was a coach and mentor. He was often found helping his children as well as many others find their way to becoming honorable adults. James taught good sportsmanship plus respect for nature and ones' fellow man.

Same story over and over – James was proving again and again he was an honorable man. His constant search for gold was a remnant of a long forgotten debt he felt he owed. But in truth James was seeking to redeem his lost honor.

Ironically, the debt occurred because James felt honor-bound to deliver his shipment, even though he did not steal it. The gold did not belong to the Spanish king. It belonged to the Aztec people. And maybe, this is why gold was, and still is, so elusive for James – the jaguar still has his paws on the treasure.

But the true treasure was in the journey, the journey to discover his humanity. His honor was and always will be in his humanity toward his fellow men. Nothing he could find, but something he has to learn.

Maybe it was no accident Quetzalcoatl was involved. Maybe this Aztec god wanted James to spend some time in self reflection.

Just as a side note, the Spanish Don, Francisco, was also on the privateer ship and was Louis in the Klondike. He too had his lessons to learn and chose to learn them with James at his side. I wonder who Francisco is in James' life today and if he too is still searching for gold?

CHAPTER 8:

TEACHERS COME IN STRANGE DISGUISES

What would you do to protect someone you love?

I've heard stories of mothers performing miraculous feats of strength by lifting cars to get their children out; teachers putting themselves between students and crazed gunmen; people jumping on grenades. Throughout history humans have shown they can be tremendously protective.

But could you, or would you, do the same things to help another soul learn one of their lessons? How far would you go?

I never would have guessed – so that's probably why I had to be shown.

Love and worry. Do we not worry about the ones we love? Sometimes? When you hear of an accident, does your mind not jump to your family and friends?

I always found it weird that my husband *never* worries about me.

When I worked night shift at a hospital where stabbings, overdoses, and gang violence were common place, it didn't bother him.

When a drug addict broke into an area where I worked alone, it didn't faze him.

When my children and I stumbled across a trapper's cabin that was used by a drug dealer, was he concerned? No. Worried? No. My father had a fit, but it didn't even get a raised eyebrow from my husband.

I was brought up with one extreme, my father, and now live with the absolute opposite. Maybe that's why I found his attitude so strange – but not strange enough to investigate. It simply bugged me when other people pointed it out and my husband would say, "Why worry? I know she can take care of herself."

One night I was watching a television episode of *Person of Interest* titled "Baby Blue", and something weird happened. Something that would force me to take a closer look at this unexplored part of my relationship.

The main character, Reece, was locked in a refrigerated truck with a small baby. Elias would kill both of them unless Reece revealed where Elias' nemesis was hiding. As the temperature dropped, Reece held the innocent baby tight in his arms. Not willing to let it die, he finally gave in and told Elias what he wanted to know.

After that show, I spiraled downward for three days straight. I couldn't eat (even chocolate), didn't sleep, didn't want to spend time with people, and didn't even go to the gym. I had no idea what was wrong or why I felt so numb.

When I finally started to analyze things, I realized there was something that wanted to be discovered, and I wasn't going forward without figuring it out. And it had all started after I watched that particular scene.

I was in Nazi Germany. I was very petite and unfortunately a very pretty young woman. The Nazi Party had enhanced its propaganda to the youth, and the Hitler Youth group had grown extensively in the preceding few years. These young soldiers terrorized the streets of Germany and my home town.

I was married and had a small daughter when I caught the eye of a group of these soldiers who had graduated into the armed forces, the SS division (the Protection Squadron). The war had not started, so there were many men who worked and trained in the area.

The oldest and ring leader of the group was named Klaus. According to him, I was his property, and no one else in the group was allowed to touch me. My husband put up with Klaus' attention to me and warned me not to anger the soldiers for they could easily have us all sent away claiming we were enemies of the Reich.

Surprisingly Klaus' attention provided us with a kind of warped protection from the other youth in the area. But I knew it was only a matter of time until his frustration came out, and it would be aimed at me.

One evening after drinking with his buddies, Klaus had been ribbed enough. They teased him about being infatuated by a woman who led him around by the nose like a puppy in heat. His frustration had peaked that night, and as predicted things got very bad.

Klaus barged into our home with the cheers of his friends behind him. He told them to leave and to take my spineless husband with them. As my husband was pulled from the bed and taken from the house, Klaus backed me into the den. Overcome with lust and drink, he attempted to rape me on the desk. My clothes were a torn mess when my daughter came crying into the room. As I looked in his eyes, I knew my daughter, who was almost ten, would be next.

I screamed for my daughter to run and hide. Then as fierce as a wild animal, I took the letter opener from the desk and slashed Klaus beyond recognition. With my bare hands, I destroyed this man, a trained soldier at least twice my size.

As the gravity of the situation took hold, there was only one thing for me to do – run. I grabbed my daughter and what clothes and food we could carry and fled. We travelled to the edge of town to a small forest where a resistance group hid. We never looked back. We never found out what happened to my husband, but heard rumors that he was blamed for Klaus' death. If that was the case, his life would not have ended well.

As I found myself back in the present, I was stunned that a simply television scene could trigger such a memory. What would you do to protect an innocent – especially if that innocent was *your* child?

I thought that was the end, the horror was over – when one final connection flickered through my mind. Klaus was my current husband, the father of my children and the man I love.

I was blindsided. I never saw *that* coming. I felt devastated, betrayed, and utterly lost.

Where did that leave me?

How in the world could Karma or destiny or whatever you call it – be so cruel?

I knew I had killed my husband in past lives, and he had killed me, but the life in Nazi Germany was so violent and so cruel – it seemed impossible that I would ever choose to love that man.

Finally, I pulled myself out of the shock and asked, "Why? Why did I need to know this? What is the meaning of this? What is the lesson?"

The pieces slowly and incredibly came together.

The reason my husband never worried about me was because he knew he didn't need to. He had cared so much about me that he took on a horrible role and died violently at a young age to show me that I could protect myself.

Who else would I have trusted with such a difficult role and such an important lesson to help me learn? The only one I would trust is him – this man I love. He protected me in that life, right up to the point where he showed me I could protect myself.

For many people my husband's blatant and continual disregard for my safety would have been ample cause to end the marriage. Obviously he didn't care. Didn't you think the same thing, as you read my description of him in the beginning of this chapter?

But with this new information, this new insight into the history and reason behind his behaviour, everything changed. It was irrefutable to me that he sacrificed his life for me, and a lot more, to help me in my journey. He always did care – far beyond this life and far beyond anything I would have ever imagined.

Our marriage and our bond are stronger than ever. Who would have thought? The pieces were pretty damning by themselves, but when put together, the finished puzzle was truly amazing.

How far would you go?

CHAPTER 9:

KARMIC DEBT

"I would die for you!" What an introduction. And he wasn't even trying to ask me out. He was my new client.

I suppose I don't corner the market on bizarre first impressions, but thank goodness, I don't blurt things out when they pop into my mind. As strange as his comment was, I don't know how he would have taken my response – "And you *have* died for me, numerous times."

I believe many of my clients and I have crossed paths in past lives. There was no doubt Robert and I had met before. Even though he was not in my office for a past life session and I didn't know if he even believed in them – I knew that we both knew – we were connected.

The spark of recognition reflected in the panic on his face as he quickly tried to back pedal out of the awkward situation. "I mean, that is...if anybody needed me to...I would. That's just who I am." We both laughed, but that weird moment of *knowing* will always stick with me.

Karma comes up in several of the classes I teach, but it definitely seems to have prevalence in past lives. Robert, like many individuals, was dealing with karmic debt.

Karmic debt is when a soul feels they owe another for something that has happened in a past life. It often comes across as something they just have to do or as Robert stated it's just who they are.

One problem with karmic debt is that the individuals do not remember *why* they owe the debt and have no idea when things are even. For example, if I did something bad, how many good deeds would it take to pay it off? Or if you did something good for me, how do I pay that back? What and how much can make things even?

It is all about perception. The soul perceives they owe a debt, and their perception is all that matters when it comes to repaying that debt.

Another problem with Karmic debt is that people around you have no idea why you are acting the way you are. For example, your spouse has that *friend*. No matter how poorly he treats your spouse, your spouse always bails him out. From giving him money, to helping him move, getting him a job, whatever it is, it just goes on and on. An endless pit. Your spouse may even put family responsibilities in second place to helping this *friend* out.

As you can imagine, this can cause big problems in relationships, especially since the constant giving often seems unjustified. By figuring out what is going on, the soul can see the whole picture and break the cycle. This allows them and maybe even the *friend* to let go and move on.

When Robert finally confessed his real reason for coming to see me, we began searching his past lives for answers. He constantly found people to help. Like a magnet – if anyone needed anything, he was there. But his latest cause was the last straw for his wife and was about to cost him his marriage. He had to understand. He wanted to find the why?

The blood, dirt, and death were palpable in the air. Robert found himself fighting with three of his closest friends among the carnage of a primitive battlefield. Most of the soldiers used swords or blades of various lengths and strengths. But there were also farmers and townspeople who had joined the fray to protect their lands. These men carried whatever they had, from sticks to slings to stones.

The four friends were soldiers. They had various weapons and seemed to work as a group when fighting. Some used close range weapons and others used longer range ones. Robert's weapon of choice was a long sword which he wielded like an extension of his own arm.

Not many used such a long sword. Most could not hold its weight, but Robert found it extremely effective when he worked in a group. It was lethal against running enemies but sometimes it took time to dislodge from an enemy's body because of its length. Therefore, Robert also carried a shorter two-foot sword for closer quarter combat.

Unfortunately, this day fate stepped in and used his favourite weapon against him. He had struck an enemy with the hilt of his long sword but it got caught under the other man's weight as he fell. In the chaos, Robert left his long sword and used his shorter blade to fight beside his friend Magnus. It was Robert's job to cover Magnus' back.

In a moment, that lasted an eternity, the fallen man got up and charged Magnus with the heavy sword. Robert leaped between them and was skewered through and through. When he fell, Magnus caught him. They both went down. There was blood everywhere.

Unbeknownst to Robert, he was not the only victim. He had thought to save Magnus but all he accomplished was to die first as the sword went through his body and into his friend. Robert died in Magnus' dying arms. Neither of them made it off the battlefield that day.

In the next life we saw, Robert was a nine-year-old Native American girl called Una. She lived in a small village that moved with the migrating buffalo herds.

"The horses are coming!" Una cried as she searched the group for her father. He had come back safe but they had no luck hunting this time. The hunting party had been gone for two days and was tired and frustrated. But the women and children were happy to have them back.

Things were becoming more difficult. Food was scarce, and friction between tribes was escalating. Thank goodness the river was nearby, and they could still fish for a while before the snow fell and the small river froze.

As a young girl, Una spent much of her time learning the tasks woman needed to know. However, she always found time to play with the children of the village and her baby brother. Looking after the children was an important role for the younger girls in the tribe. It gave the older women time to get other things done, like mending, washing, cooking, and preparing food to be stored for the winter.

Robert enjoyed this life, but there seemed to be so much worry in one so young. He could feel Una's anxiety when the men left and her relief when they returned. Even if they brought no food, the little girl knew it was better when the men were with the tribe – it was safer.

The connection between Robert and this girl was extremely evident. As he relived the last hours of Una's life, the strong man in my office became very emotional. "She was so young and didn't know better," he kept saying.

As the scene unfolded, the carnage was revealed. Everyone was dead. The entire village, massacred.

Early that morning, the men had gone out to hunt. But by early afternoon horses were heard returning. It was strange for them to come back so soon. Something must be wrong. As the villagers came out to see what was happening, they realized it was not their men returning. It was a raid from a neighbouring tribe. The raiders had come to steal women and food from the village for their own.

They would kill all the old women and young boys and anyone who resisted or caused trouble.

Una did not resist, so why did she die? Robert reluctantly watched as a painted brave on a horse came blazing towards Una's baby brother. The small child just stood there, frozen in fear. The girl ran to push her brother out of harm's way and was trampled by the horse. As Una died in her brothers arms, the brave came back and slit the boy's throat.

Again, they died together. Robert was the young girl and the brother was his old friend Magnus. Many times Robert had tried to save his friend, and every time he failed, lifetime after lifetime. Why?

We needed to find the cause. When and where did this cycle begin? We traveled back to one last life, back to where the *debt* occurred.

This time I found and told the story. Robert had struggled with the little girl's death, and I knew revealing the cause would be even more emotional for him.

As before, we found Robert in a horrible place. It was a filthy, rat-infested dungeon, and the rancid smell of blood, sweat, and urine was overpowering. As I approached a pile of rags in the corner of the cell, I knew it was Robert.

A young woman lay on the floor, but she was almost unrecognizable. Her hair was matted and filled with lice and feces. Dried blood and vomit crusted on her face and clothes. Beaten and thrown here like garbage, she looked so deathly pale, but a small movement revealed she was still alive. And – that she was pregnant.

We needed to go further back in time to learn the story behind this horrific scene.

Eight months prior, this girl had a very different life. She was a young maid named Maria who had just started working in a local baron's manor. The work was hard, and she spent most of the time in the kitchens. One evening Maria was told to help serve the meal because another maid had taken ill. This night changed everything for Maria.

As she carried heavy platters to the table, her graceful movements and carefree smile belied her difficult past. These qualities were not missed by the baron's son, who quickly decided to take her for his own.

The baron's son, Nicolas, was infatuated with the maid. He courted Maria as if she were born of his station. One night they had a secret rendezvous where he spoke of his undying love and how one day they would marry. That's when their love affair began.

They had a blissful month of stolen moments and steamy nights. Maria was special, and Nicolas wanted to make sure she felt cherished. He would give her small tokens and speak of the life they would one day share. Life was grand.

Unfortunately, the Baroness found out. She knew her son was experienced with women, but she quickly realized this was more than mere infatuation. Nicolas had a responsibility to his family. He had to marry well, and it had to be a girl who would contribute to the family's status. So the Baroness created a plan to temporarily get her son out of the palace so she could put an end to this unacceptable affair.

Nicolas was too naive to even suspect anything was amiss. The Baroness said her daughter needed to meet some suitable men. As the older brother, Nicolas was sent to act as chaperone. They went to Madrid, on very important family business: to find his sister a husband. The two siblings were gone for almost six months, but despite the balls and parties and all the time apart, Nicolas never forgot Maria.

Maria didn't forget Nicolas either, for while he was away, Maria discovered she was carrying his child. She hid the fact for a long time as she desperately prayed her beloved would return and marry her as promised. Again, the Baroness found out first.

It was relatively easy to get rid of people in those days, but Nicolas's generosity made it even easier. All the Baroness had to do was tell her husband that some of her jewelry was missing, and he would search the servants' quarters. Nicolas's tokens to Maria would be found, and the Baroness would claim they were hers. Then Maria could be executed for thievery.

As the Baroness planned, the Baron discovered the jewelry, but he also discovered Maria was pregnant. He declared the pregnancy was her motive for stealing. Since she was unwed and would have lost her position in the household, this was Maria's desperate solution to provide for her child. They were lucky to catch her before she stole everything from them and fled the area.

Trying to tell them the truth about the child only enraged the Baron, to the point where he had Maria whipped until she confessed the child was not his son's. Those were the only words the Baron wanted to hear, the only truth he would accept. There was no way he would accept a servant's bastard as his grandchild and heir. Maria was simply lying in hopes of saving her life and the life of the child. It was not going to work. The Baron had her confession, and that was all he would tell his son when Nicolas returned from Madrid, if his son even asked.

There was no hope for Maria. Nicolas was not coming, and if he did, what would he think of her now? Things had gone terribly wrong. Maria was about to let go of this life when a cloaked figure came to her cell. It was Nicolas's nurse maid from when he was a child. The woman had bribed the guards to let her see the girl. Maria had met her several times and suspected she knew of Nicolas's affair. Now Maria thanked God, the nurse had known.

A deal was to be created that night, but first a painful decision had to be made. The woman could not save Maria, but she could save the child. The child was big enough to take from the womb but the girl would die in the delivery.

The nurse promised to see the child raised by her sister who had just lost a child of her own. She also promised to pad the girl's stomach to look as if she were still with child when they found her dead in the cell. No one would know, but the baby would survive.

And that is exactly what happened. The girl survived long enough to name her male child, a strong name, after a strong man, her grandfather – Magnus.

As this young girl drew her final breath, her biggest regret was leaving the child alone to fend for himself. Maria knew what it was like to be alone in the world. It was unfair especially for a child. She wished she could stay with him and give him the life he deserved. A mother should not have to leave her son to strangers. She wanted so much to stay with him and have a wonderful life together as a family – her, the child, and Nicolas. But that was not their fate.

The boy grew up to have a good life and even got to know his real father but only as friends. One thing, however, haunted Magnus. He always remembered the story his adopted mother told him as she died. It was the sad tale of his birth and his true parentage.

His true mother had sacrificed everything for him, including her life. Maria's last thoughts and dreams were of him with the hope he would live a life filled with love. Magnus never understood that kind of unconditional love. He never experienced it. The one thing he had learned throughout that life, however, was that you have to repay your debts. He owed his mother everything and never got a chance to repay her. Somehow, someway, he swore he would.

As we looked back over the story, the truth hit us with unforeseen clarity. Even though we knew Robert had been in that cell, only now did we realize – he was not the girl – he was the unborn child. Robert was the baby and the mother was the first Magnus and the little native girl's brother.

But what did it all mean?

Was Robert destined to repeat the cycle until his mother had a good life? Robert kept trying to save her, but every time they died together. Would saving her break the cycle? Was it truly a karmic debt that had to be repaid?

That seemed too simple – what about the lesson to be learned? The key is always in the lesson as it is in this story as well.

Maria's last wish for her son was for him to be loved and to know a love like she had for him. A love so strong it was more important than self preservation. That was the lesson Robert kept trying to learn but always missed.

Robert had described his duty to die in battle, his duty to protect his comrades, and his duty to fight for the cause. Everything was about duty. His sacrifice hadn't been born out of love for a friend but out of his sense of duty.

Una, the native girl, had described her responsibility to look after the children of the tribe. Her responsibility. Again in that life, Una's sacrifice hadn't been out of love for the brother but out of a sense of responsibility.

Robert had wrapped his sense of debt with the lesson he was to learn, possibly hoping to accomplish both. I believe the true debt Robert has is to find love and be willing to sacrifice everything for that love. Only then will he have the life his mother wished for him. Only then would he be free of this cycle. Not *dying* for the other, but living for them.

In this life Robert is still desperately seeking causes to die for. He constantly tries to help people, often out of very dangerous situations. He is more than willing to "die for you," but he has not yet found anyone to live for.

Did Robert truly hear and understand this lesson? I am not sure. I can only hope one day he will find that kind of love – find his happy ending.

CHAPTER 10:

SOUL MATES

Wolves mate for life. Swans mate for life. How come it seems so hard for humans?

People are fascinated by the concept of soul mates, and are always asking me questions. What is a soul mate? Am I married to my soul mate? Do you need to find your soul mate to be happy? Is that what makes a relationship last? How do you know if someone is your soul mate? Can we have more than one?

Souls enjoy playing with some souls more than others. They create deep bonds of trust and friendship within a smaller group. Often these souls go through many lives together with the intention of helping each other learn their lessons more easily and more efficiently.

Even though these soul groups often spend numerous lives together, that does not mean their roles remain the same. Sometimes one particular soul may have a large part in one life and a more limited part in another. There are major roles and minor roles, but in general we spend time with between six to ten other souls on a regular basis.

Therefore, we have multiple soul "mates" – or friends. And like parents with children we love them all. One child is key at one time of life and a different child may be key at another. And sometimes we choose not to play with our regular friends at all. We want to be alone.

Sarah traveled across the world to find her soul mate. There was no question in her mind that is exactly who he was.

Africa always fascinated Sarah. She dreamt of going on safari and seeing the interesting animals. When she was a child, Sarah read *in National Geographic* about a little island off the coast of Kenya, and since then it has been her mental sanctuary. She pictured how the people lived and how peaceful it must be. Whenever life became overwhelming, Sarah would go to the little island in her mind and find peace.

Unfortunately, getting there physically proved to be much more challenging. Every time she got close to going, something would happen to prevent it. Sometimes family responsibilities or financial issues stopped her. Other times she couldn't get time off work. And even if everything else worked out, she had no one to travel with, and she didn't want to go alone.

Sarah's life had become a stagnant cycle. Nothing worked out like she hoped. Nothing was hugely wrong, but nothing was wonderfully right either. Work was work. Family and friends were busy. Her relationship with her boyfriend was old. And her dream vacation was on hold – again. Her life was boring. If this was all life had to offer, Hollywood definitely lied about romance and adventure.

It is funny how when you're on the verge of giving up, everything suddenly lines up. For instance when a couple finally decides to adopt, they become pregnant. Well Sarah was there, on the cusp.

Her boyfriend wanted to go to Mexico, and Sarah decided to appease him. Maybe it would spark the now totally extinguished flame. When an associate at work mentioned that Mexico would be nice, to her surprise Sarah replied, "Nice – like a root canal."

Sarah told Christine, her friend from work, that nothing would ever come close to her dream of going to Africa. Christine listened compassionately as Sarah expressed, in vivid detail, her deepest desire. Then finally, near tears, Sarah declared, "But it's only a dream – it will never come true."

Christine felt the passion, longing, and defeat in Sarah's voice. Then it happened – a simple, surprising statement that changed everything. "Heck, I'll go with you."

Sarah was shocked. She had not known Christine long but here Christine was volunteering to go on her adventure, half way across the world just because Sarah wanted to go.

Once Christine convinced Sarah she was serious, all the details whirled into place. They both got four weeks off and a discount on flights. Everything was set.

I tell people, when something is supposed to happen, all obstacles tend to fade away. The path becomes effortless. So if you are struggling to get something, someone, or somewhere, stop. Your path should flow. That does not mean you sit and do nothing. You must take action, but the action should feel surprisingly unforced.

Sarah and Christine arrived in Nairobi and traveled south to a game reserve. It was very hot and extremely dry. Driving was rough and their luggage was covered in layers of dust. Bugs were everywhere and in everything. And Sarah had never been happier.

After the safari, they spent some time in Mombasa. The last four days of their trip, they planned to visit the small island off the coast. Sarah would finally see the place she had imagined for so many years. Christine was a little hesitant to take the small boat across to the isolated island. But after coming so far, Sarah could not leave without visiting her island.

The island was small enough to walk from one end to the other in a couple hours. It had a few shops and restaurants, and the beaches were naturally peaceful. The island was not a regular tourist location, so when you walked through the little village, it felt like stepping back in time.

The first day Sarah and Christine walked to the far side of the island, and on the way back decided to stop at one of the restaurants for something cold to drink. One in particular – a dark, reclusive shop – called to Sarah. Christine thought Sarah was crazy.

When they entered, they noticed the only seats were at the bar or far in the back. Christine's mind ran every horrifying scenario. Were they asking for trouble? Had they come all this way to be murdered, where no one would ever find them? Or maybe they would be lucky and not killed – just sold into white slavery.

Sarah didn't notice a thing. When she walked through the doorway of the dark little bar, on an isolated island, off the coast of Africa, half way around the world – Sarah found her soul mate.

"It was like in the movies," Sarah said. "As our eyes met, the room grew quiet. Sparks flew. There was an instant connection. We were the only two people in existence for that second. That heartbeat that lasted an eternity."

Just listening to her, I got goose bumps and could feel the electricity as all the hair on my arms stood on end.

They spent three glorious days together – doing nothing.

Kobe was in a marriage that never should have happened but he couldn't seem to end it. His wife lived on the mainland while he spent most of his time on the island. He had lived there all his life, built his restaurant, and ran it for most of his adult life. He wasn't happy, but he wasn't unhappy either. This was just his life.

Sarah and Kobe didn't discuss the future, but they did exchange e-mail addresses so they could keep in touch.

On the day Sarah and Christine were leaving, Kobe came to the boat to see Sarah one last time. He wanted to give her something. Something special that would remind her of him and their time together. After much deliberation he found the perfect gift.

"I have a gift for you," he smiled proudly. But his expression changed when he realized, "But I forgot it."

As he ran back to his shop he yelled, "Don't leave, I will be right back."

Sarah waited. Knots in her stomach grew as their luggage was loaded. Her face turned white when they were instructed to board the boat. And her heart ached when the captain informed them it was time to leave. They could wait no longer.

There were no goodbyes. No hug. No kiss. No promises. No tears. All she had was an unspoken hope that they would keep in touch.

When Sarah came to see me, we discussed what had happened.

Why was her soul mate half way around the world? Sarah definitely was not going to give up her high paced, high tech world to step back in time. And how realistic was it to expect Kobe to give up the life he knew to live in Canada. Sarah didn't know what to do.

Since I am always looking for the underlying story or cause, I posed a couple of questions. This took the discussion in a different direction and forced Sarah to look at the situation in a new way.

"Why would you and Kobe choose to live this life worlds apart with almost zero chances of ever meeting?" I asked. "And if the point was to keep you apart in this life, why did you meet at all?"

The answer to the second question was much easier to see. For as soon as Sarah got off the plane, she broke up with her boyfriend. She took one look at him and realized there was more to love than this. Their relationship had been nice and convenient. She liked him a lot, but now she knew love should be bigger. Hollywood had known something after all.

Love is hard to put into words. Just remember, if you have to ask, "Is this it?" – then it's not. No rationalizing. No qualifying. If you're asking the question – it simply isn't.

Sarah now realized, she did not love her boyfriend. She had not really loved any of them. Nothing she had experienced, thus far in her life, compared to the depth of her feelings for Kobe.

Everything changed. After meeting Kobe, Sarah figured out love is real. It's out there. It's not simply worth waiting for – it's worth hunting for.

Like a predator in Africa, go out there and find it. Don't give up until you are enjoying the spoils of your efforts.

Sarah knew she would never settle for less again.

But now what? Was she supposed to make it work with Kobe? Or was she suppose to pine for him for the rest of her life? He never said he would divorce his wife. They never discussed any future together.

Having answered the question of why they met, now we had to look at the question of why they put themselves so far apart. The chances of meeting were so slim — why? If they are soul mates and meant to be together, why make it virtually impossible to connect?

We looked at their pasts. It became clear that Sarah and Kobe shared many previous lives. In fact they were in a group of six souls who journeyed together.

In all their lives Sarah and Kobe were very similar in character. The group often got into trouble, and these two always had to get them out of it — or at least try. Numerous times Sarah and Kobe had sacrificed themselves to save the others.

In one life they were prisoners in Australia, which was a British penal colony. They were incarcerated for political protests and disruptions they caused in England. Being no less vocal in Australia, they often got into violent clashes with other inmates.

Interestingly, even though Sarah and Kobe were the quietest of the group, they usually got the punishment. When several of the group members managed to escape, it was these two, once again, who paid the price. This time, however, they would make the ultimate sacrifice.

As the group crossed a wide river pursued by guards and dogs, a crocodile took after them. Kobe left his friends to lure the croc away. Sarah went back to help him, and neither of them survived the attack. The rest of the group didn't stop, and they all escaped.

In another life, four of the group were cattle rustlers. Kobe had grown up with these men, and unfortunately when thefts were discovered nearby, Kobe got blamed. In the eyes of the townspeople, he was part of the gang — guilt by association.

Kobe sat bravely atop his favorite horse. As they were about to put the noose around his neck, Sarah rode into town, guns firing. No one would be hanging her brother today.

She was right – they both got shot. Then, as a warning to others – their bodies were displayed on the road into town. Neither of them were part of the gang.

Many times the group got Sarah and Kobe in trouble. And every time Kobe ended up getting Sarah killed. As I watched yet another death scene, an important piece of the puzzle came to light.

Sarah and Kobe were lying in the dirt dying – again. He held her in his mangled arms and, using the last of his strength, finally declared, "No more. I can't stand to see you die because of me anymore."

Sometimes souls decide to not play with each other for a while. Sometimes there are things they need to learn before they can be together again. And sometimes they are better off apart.

Kobe made a painful decision – to stay away from Sarah. She was not happy about it and tried to offer alternatives, more options. But they had already tried numerous times to change the ending. They tried different stories, different places, and different times – and he always caused her death. So grudgingly, for this life, Sarah finally agreed to stay away from Kobe and the whole group.

Trying to be true to her promise, Sarah made very few friends and has no one she considers really close. Her family is not tight knit, and she has no children or even a pet. In this life she is not part of a group or constantly protecting another – she is finding out who she is.

It is not easy for Sarah to focus on herself. She often tries to find causes – people who need her help and her sacrifice. As we looked back, most of her relationships were the same. She was always trying to save a guy from something – addiction, financial troubles, bad relationships. You name it, she'd try to save them from it, even from themselves.

How did finding Kobe really change Sarah in this life?

It was a reminder.

"Remember me? Remember us?" his soul yelled. "We decided to be apart – but only until we learnt what we are supposed to. Have you forgotten? Or do you want to spend forever apart? What are you doing wasting this life doing the same things all over again? Remember our deal! Get to work, or we will never be together again."

When Sarah finally heard the message, things in this life really started changing. This life was set up for her to discover herself, to find relationships where she can develop and blossom. That does not mean she can't help others, but it has to be more mutually beneficial, not just her always giving and the other person always taking.

Many relationships are one sided because of lessons that are supposed to be learned. But for Sarah, she needs to learn give and take – balance. I have seen many souls do a complete turnaround and switch from all giving to all taking or vise-versa, but eventually they all need to learn balance.

It was humorous to see how Sarah tried to remind herself to learn this lesson.

She has a yin-yang symbol tattooed on her hip. Her vehicles have always been white with black interior. She is Caucasian but has always dated African American men. She works in a man's world but dresses very feminine. The examples go on and on. Balance.

Sarah had gotten off track. Fortunately, she's back on it. She just needed a not-so-subtle reminder.

She has found a new man who adds spark and balance to her life. And no, it is not Kobe. She realized that meeting him in this life was just to put her on the right path again. Who knows, maybe if it all works out, they can be together again in another life, sooner rather than later. Or maybe she will discover a new set of soul mates that she wants to know better.

Just because souls play within a given group does not mean they cannot branch out to other groups. Just because souls have special relationships with others in one life does not mean they must be together for eternity. Sometimes souls choose to be apart for growth. Sometimes they're bored.

Sharing lives make very special bonds. Enjoy them. Acknowledge them, especially when you meet "a soul mate". But remember this – you can have more than one special relationship in each life, let alone across multiple lives. There is a plan, and as long as you continue forward and don't dwell in the past, all kinds of wonderful things are possible.

CHAPTER 11:

UNANSWERED PRAYERS

"Why are we here?" Laura asked the rhetorical question once again. She and her uncle had been sitting in the rain, in the dark, for four hours. Worse — they had done it for seven nights in a row.

Her uncle told her hundreds of times, they had to wait. She knew the importance of their mission, but that didn't make it any easier. The waiting had become too much for her. Laura had always been impatient, but this verged on torture.

Two nights before, the Germans had brought a young soldier to this location, no older than her. Now they carried him out on a stretcher. He had been beaten so badly he couldn't walk. Laura barely recognized him through the bruises and bandages on his face. It appeared they had broken his nose as well as his right arm.

"We could have stopped this." Laura felt helpless. "He did not have to go through any of this. What are we here for if we can't help — can't stop these mad men from butchering our people, our soldiers? What is our purpose? Why are we here?"

Laura's questions transcend time. Individuals have pondered their role in the human existence for millenniums. Are we getting any closer to the answers? That's debatable, but sometimes we get a peek at the big picture.

Laura had been asking similar questions for many lives, and in this life all her questions centered on a guy she met and lost – literally. It started with the small picture, but in the end – she got a glimpse of something much larger.

"It was like we had known each other before. There was such an intense connection." Laura told me how they met, and I must admit, it appeared pretty obvious where this was heading – but it never got there. I can see why she got so frustrated.

They were thrown together on a joint project, but they worked for two different companies, in two different provinces. They were to coordinate a big seminar that overlapped corporate boundaries. When they finally met at the event after months of preparation, there was an instant attraction.

She was happily married, and he was going through a messy divorce and custody battle. When they met at the event – nothing happened. No, I don't get to write a steamy love scene yet.

All that happened was a wonderful evening of light conversation. They were like two friends who hadn't seen each other for many years. But they definitely had chemistry. Neither of them dared take the next step. They were too scared. One wrong move – or maybe one right move – and they would be consumed by the underlying flame.

But not that night. Or any other night, for that matter – and that was the problem.

It's interesting that when we don't get something we want, or something doesn't turn out quite right, we go back to that fundamental question. What is my purpose in life?

After that night a strange series of events left Laura stranded. The two promised to stay in touch, but she suddenly quit her job, and as coincidental as it may seem, so did he. Now she had no way of contacting him. She only knew his work e-mail and the town he lived in. Since she had given him her home e-mail, all she could do was wait and hope he would contact her. So she waited, and waited, and waited.

And then she came to see me.

Laura was full of those big questions. Why did I meet him if we weren't supposed to be together? There must be more to life that just waiting and wondering. What am I suppose to do now? Am I supposed to chase him? Do I want to?

As much as she tried, she couldn't stop thinking about him. There was more to how she felt than physical attraction. She needed to understand it. She needed to know where this connection came from – so back we went.

Laura was the daughter of a very influential business man in Europe in the 1930s. Her parents doted on her and sent her to a distinguished school away from home. While she was away, the local church in her home town was bombed. Her parents and older brother all perished in the attack. The only family Laura had left was an uncle in a small town in the center of France.

World War II had just begun, and Laura found herself joining her uncle in the resistance. In the beginning, her role was quite small, but before long she was playing a major part in many of their clandestine escapades. Women could get a lot more information than men, and her being young and beautiful didn't hurt their success either.

Laura was young and naive. She hated waiting, hated having no control, and really hated watching people get tortured by the Nazis. But as her uncle had repeatedly told her, they could not blow up the warehouse – yet.

When he saw the helpless look on Laura's face, he tried to emphasize the importance of their mission once again. "Our assignment is clear. We have to wait for a specific prisoner and get him out. He carries information vital for the war effort, and we have to get him back to England. If we bombed this warehouse now, the Germans would just move their interrogation site somewhere else, and it may take months to find the new location. Ending the war is the only way to end this madness and save all our soldiers."

Laura didn't like the answer, but she understood. So they waited.

It was late May when the German soldiers brought a hooded man into the warehouse. Though it was dark, the moon shone just enough to reflect on the British insignia the prisoner wore. He had Royal Air Force (RAF) wings just above his left shirt pocket. Finally, this was the one. He was the pilot, the flyboy they were waiting for.

Word reached the group of resistance, and Laura finally got her chance to act. The plan had been set for weeks, and they just had to pray everything went according to it.

Three young boys would distract the front guards while the main group launched smoke bombs through the windows on the front and two sides of the main building. Prisoners were held in the back room with direct access to the rear exit. As the main attack force stormed the front and sides of the building, guards would take the prisoner out the back – right into the ambush Laura and her uncle would have waiting for them.

It went like clockwork. Only two guards came out the back, and the prisoner was smart enough to realize it was a rescue attempt. He was ready when his chance came and quickly fell into step behind Laura as they entered the woods. The main group distracted the soldiers long enough for the three to make their way safely to the rendezvous point. The worst was over.

The leaders of her group and the British captain, MacBurie, spent most of the night discussing their next move. They had to get him to the English Channel. From there another branch of the resistance would take him across and back to London. Mac, as he was known, had vital information the Allied Air Force desperately needed.

Before daybreak, Laura and Mac headed north with Sebastien, a scout from their group. If all went well, it would take them just over two weeks to get to the Channel by foot. Since Laura was known in these areas and female, it would be much easier for her to get food and lodging for the group. All precautions were to be taken. Caution took precedence over speed. The Allies would never get the information if Mac died on his way back.

On their journey Sebastien only had eyes for Laura, but Laura only had eyes for Mac. Maybe that was why her uncle sent Sebastien with them, to make sure she came home.

Mac was in his late twenties and had a family somewhere in England. The two had been childhood friends, and married just before he left for service. Shortly after training camp, he received news that he was the father of a darling baby girl. That had been almost three years before, and he'd never been back.

Laura and Mac had a strange bond. It was as if they had known each other much longer than the mere weeks they had been travelling together. Sebastien saw what was happening but was a realist. Mac was going home, and Laura would be staying in France. He would get his chance. He just had to be patient.

As the group got closer to Le Havre and their final destination, sadness darkened Laura's heart. Even though Mac had vowed to come back to her, there was a feeling —almost foreboding— growing in her soul.

Mac left. There were no tears or drama, just a final, "Be safe," and he was gone.

When Laura and Sebastien finally got back to her uncle's, activity for the resistance was intensifying. Her days were busy, and she spent all her spare time helping to plan raids and sabotage attacks. Laura tried hard not to think about Mac, but she was anxious to know if he was safe or at the least to know if he had made it across the deadly English Channel.

Finally, word made it back to their group that Mac had indeed made his way across the Channel and back to London. The information he carried must have been correct because the bombing raids became more frequent and considerably more successful. The war seemed to be turning in their favor, but with it the Germans were becoming more desperate and more violent.

Nights were the worst. Allied raiders would use the cover of darkness to mask their approach, lighting up the sky with their artillery and bombing attacks. The night raids were more and more frequent and often went on for weeks, hitting various targets within the occupied zone.

Lying awake in her cot, Laura listened to the distant bombardment as her room lit up with flashes of yellow and orange. As she drifted off in an exhausted sleep, she would hear the planes overhead. She would dream, and wait. She was constantly waiting, drifting between hope and despair.

Sebastien waited as well, knowing that one day he would get his chance. And finally one day when the war ended and Mac had still not returned, Sebastien's wait was over. Laura and Sebastien were married, and several years later had a daughter of their own.

Laura never forgot, but never tried to find Mac. She envisioned him with his family, living happily, having forgotten all about her. Maybe her feelings were just a girl's infatuation like Sebastien had said. But every time she heard a plane, she thought of him.

Unbeknownst to Laura, happily ever after was not in the cards for Mac. He had kept his word and come back for her. There was a dangerous mission to sneak across enemy territory into unoccupied France and help coordinate a major Allied attack with the resistance. Mac volunteered. Because of his knowledge of the area and language, his familiarity with many members of the resistance, plus his being a combat pilot, Mac was the RAF's first choice.

Laura should have been aware of the resistance's plan to bring Mac back, but the German SS had stirred things up in her area, and the communication was patchy at best. Mac was supposed to land in the southwest of France and make his way north. But word never got through that he was coming. His plane was shot down just entering France.

Mac died in that plane crash, and his last thoughts were of her. "Laura I came back for you."

But Laura never found out. She never knew what happened and never found the peace that knowing would have brought.

As we fast forwarded to her death in that life, the one regret she had was not going in search of him, not finding out what had happened and not even looking. Her last thoughts were of him. "Next time I will look for you. Even if I think it is hopeless – I will try."

As that life faded from my vision, I knew it was not the first time Laura had been left waiting or wondering about Mac. It had happened many times across many lives. And she was doing it all over again, for she now knew that Mac and the man from the project were the same soul. Again she was waiting and wondering without enough information to look.

Laura left my office that day with a new determination. She would find Mac in this life and break the cycle. But was that the real end of the story? If she found him and resolved their relationship, would that end the cycle of waiting and wondering? Was the lesson simply that you have to act to get what you want, not just sit around and wait?

That solution didn't sit quite right with me and not surprisingly, I found out later that Laura's new determination did not change her situation much either.

She couldn't find him even though she reached out to her colleagues for help. Searching and coming to another impasse did not end her longing. She still couldn't let it go.

That told me we had not found the true lesson yet. For if the answer was to do everything she could to find him – which she had – she would be able to let go. If the answer was to find him – she should have – but she didn't. Because neither of these things happened, it proved we had not discovered the underlying lesson.

It's as easy as that. If the issue does not go away – keep looking. You missed something.

Our next step was to go after the cause. We had to find the event that started the cycle in the beginning. Then we would figure out the true lesson, which would break the cycle. We hadn't gotten to the real end yet. We were simply one step closer to it. We had to get out of the story and continue the search. Many times the obvious answer is not the lesson. Look for the deeper meaning to find the actual lesson.

When we went looking for the cause, this is the life that unfolded.

In this new, earlier life Laura ran away. Similar to Kate at the end of the movie *Titanic*, Laura was lost and just walked away from her old life.

Laura was a sailor in Her Majesty's Royal Navy in the 1700s. Her name was Jacob. In a terrible storm Jacob's ship along with several others sank somewhere in the English Channel. He clung to debris for many days until a small fishing boat found him and brought him to shore. Almost dead, Jacob was taken to a village on the coast of France where he slowly recovered.

No one in the village knew Jacob's background. His clothes were torn, and he had wrapped himself in the remnants of a sail. They didn't know he was a sailor in the British navy and readily accepted him into their community. He became strong and found he had a great skill for building things with his hands. He built a home and life near the village and was always helping those around him. Jacob was at peace in this new life.

Jacob's past was far away and thankfully forgotten. All his life he was pressured to live up to society's expectations because of who he was. He had been forced into the navy by family obligations and hated it. While many of his colleagues were filled with dreams of adventure and prestige, Jacob never was. All he wanted was to have a quiet life and be able to spend time in nature. So he stayed in the small village. He was dead to his family in Britain. He could truly live in France. Life turned out exactly like he wanted, quiet and peaceful. No guilt. No remorse.

Unfortunately, not everyone was as lucky. Along with his family back in England, Jacob had left a fiancé. Her life did not turn out as well.

Jessica was always destined to marry Jacob. Even though she was much younger, the arrangement her father had made was precisely what she wanted. Jacob was the handsome firstborn son of a very well-to-do family. After his time in the navy, the couple would settle down and have a bunch of children. Jacob would spend his days working with his father at their family business, and Jessica would have her ideal life.

She would be the perfect wife and mother. Many of her days would be spent planning dinners and elaborate parties, where she would wear beautiful gowns and show off their immaculate home. Her children would be well behaved, and their nanny would ensure they were always presentable, a perfect addition to the family name. But Jessica's dreams never came true.

When Jacob's ship wrecked off the English coast, many sailors were lost at sea. The navy classified him missing and presumed dead. For months Jessica was haunted by her dreams, dreams that they had made a mistake and that Jacob was on his way home to marry her. One day she would walk into the house, and there he would be – handsome and alive as ever, declaring his love for her.

Jessica waited and waited for something, something that would give her peace of mind, some knowledge that would give her closure. They never found his body, and after several months the navy declared him dead. His family had an elegant funeral, and all the high-society attended. Then life went on.

Eventually Jessica's father arranged a new union for his daughter. She too had to move on. She would marry an influential landowner and live in the country in Northern England. There were no big parties or balls. She had to be content raising her two daughters and having a simple country life.

She never found out Jacob was living his own life in a small village across the Channel. A life strangely similar to the one she now called her own. But the biggest difference between their lives was that Jacob had found peace and Jessica never did.

In the lives that followed Jacob's life, Laura had become the person who is always waiting and wondering. She had taken on Jessica's role.

Was it Karmic payback? No, something bigger. I do not believe Karma punishes, but it does make you understand and learn. There was a lesson here, we now had to find it.

The most obvious lesson was that Laura needed to live so there would be no regrets.

On that fateful day of your death, when you look back over what you have done, you want to have no regrets. When choices come to you along you life's journey, ask yourself, "If I don't do this, will I forever wonder, 'What if'? Can I live with the unknown, never knowing what would have happened if...?"

Search if you need to search. Find your answers if you need to, or be at peace not to. Know you have done all you can do or want to do, then move on and *LIVE* your life. The wondering puts you in a hold pattern. It puts the lesson back on the shelf for you to learn another day – or another life.

Some people move on because they are forced to, but they often live differently. They live in a sense of looking for 'it' or worrying that they have already missed 'it'. There is a difference between going through life, and *living* life – when you truly participate trying to get the full experience.

This was the solution Laura had come to after the first life, the life in WWII she saw with Mac. It's a great lesson, one we kept coming back to, over and over again. But she tried it, tried to find closure, searched as much as she could, and still was left in the hold pattern.

Nothing had really changed for her, which told us that this was not the lesson she had set out to learn. So what new information could we use from the causal life to discover the true lesson? Remember the reason we go through all this is to understand and learn.

Now looking back at the causal life, we realized Laura could not understand why Jessica did not move on with her life. It was not that Jacob and Jessica were in love. They were simply connected. Jacob had a wonderful life, so why couldn't Jessica?

It was like Jacob wanted to understand, and took on that role to do just that. Jacob thought it should be easy to move on in a similar situation, as he had. But Laura has spent several lives realizing it wasn't as easy as Jacob had thought.

When Laura changed the circumstances and put herself in a life more similar to Jessica, it proved much more difficult to move on. Laura got herself stuck in a loop.

Why?

Because the lesson was not in the getting back together, which Laura has spent many lives trying to do. The lesson was in them *never* getting back together. The lesson to be learnt was – why is it easy for one person to move on when they lose someone and not for another?

When the female in Laura's lives lost the male, it was not just the person she lost. Many things were intertwined with the future she had planned with that man. It is easiest to see in Jessica's story. She had planned her whole life based around marrying Jacob. When Jacob disappeared, Jessica lost all her dreams as well. She settled for a quiet country life with her landowner husband.

When Laura was in France, she did the same. Recall her passion for action, helping others, making a difference. Her original plans did not include settling down with Sebastien and raising a child. Her parents doted on her and sent her away to school. Not because they wanted her gone but because she wanted more. She wanted to pursue an education.

Her father was a businessman, and she had ideas and plans to help. She could convince anyone to do anything for her, which was evident in the war. She could get people to help her in unoccupied as well as occupied territory, even though they would be killed if discovered. It would have been easy for her to expand her father's business with her skills, but that opportunity ended with her father's death.

With Mac she once again had options opening for her. She could go to England and have a new life. Anything was possible. When he did not return, all that ended, and she settled into a role of wife and mother.

Now to determine if this truly was the lesson we were searching for, we had to see how it fit with Laura's current life.

Unbeknownst to me, Laura always wanted to be a travel representative and fly around the world. She loved airplanes. That meant spending a lot of time away from home. But she had a husband and daughter. Her daughter was almost twenty and starting her own life, but Laura knew following her dreams would create problems in her marriage.

Laura's husband was always supportive, and a great friend, so she found every excuse not to follow her dreams. Have you guessed who her husband is yet? Her current husband is Sebastien.

Part of what she wanted was the freedom to meet new people, create new relationships, and not be held back by a previous commitment. But how could she do that to Sebastien? Secretly she knew, her dreams and her marriage were mutually exclusive. She couldn't have both.

What this mysterious man really offered Laura was a way out.

When we arrived at this conclusion, Laura realized to her shock, how true it was.

For Jacob, the storm had conveniently taken him out of Jessica's life. Jacob did not want to tell his parents and fiancé that he did not want to pursue the life they had planned for him – but he didn't have to.

For Laura in France, Mac's return would have got Sebastien out of the picture. But when Mac didn't come back, Laura did not want to break Sebastien's heart. He had been so supportive and had waited so long for her – so she didn't.

In this life, same thing. Laura did not want to hurt her husband. How could she tell him she wanted out of the marriage, so she could travel the world? But she knew if she had found her mystery man, they would have an affair. Then her husband would end the marriage for her.

So we finally discovered what the mystery man was about – but what was the lesson? Remember, Jacob wanted to understand why it was so easy for him to move on and not Jessica.

Out of all the information we've gathered, there is one key difference in Laura's lives – that convenient storm.

When Jacob couldn't figure out why Jessica didn't move on, he was missing a vital piece of information. While Jacob moved on to *follow* his dreams, he *encapsulated* Jessica's dreams. For Jessica, moving on meant leaving her dreams behind, unfulfilled. She hadn't just lost Jacob. She had lost the wonderful life she had planned.

For Jessica to get back on the path towards her dreams, she would have had some tough work to do. First she had to detangle Jacob from her dreams. Second she had to take action to steer her life toward those dreams. She had to speak up and tell her father what she wanted, and not marry the landowner in the country.

Have you guessed who Jessica is yet? Keep reading.

In the other two lives, Laura faced the same challenge. She would have had to get *herself* back on path. But Jacob didn't know that part. He let Laura wait and wait until some convenient storm came along to do it for her. And in both cases that storm was Mac. And in both cases Laura ended up in a waiting game.

Mac was to prevent Laura from marrying Sebastien in France. And the mystery man, who was also Mac, was to get Laura out of her marriage in this life. But conveniently, Mac and the mystery man got lost.

For Jacob to understand why Jessica couldn't move on, he had to recognize the important role of the storm to the story. Mac couldn't be the one to get Laura back on her path to her dreams – she had to do it herself.

It takes strength and bravery to speak up and say what you want. It takes even more when your dreams conflict with those around you. And even more still when it will hurt people you love and respect.

If you are not committed to a path, be it a relationship or a lifestyle, are you not cheating those around you? How many lives has Sebastien lived being second choice? Maybe if Laura gave her husband a chance in this life, he would find someone who truly wanted to be with him. Maybe he has put dreams on hold to be with Laura. Maybe by cutting the connection, they would both be better off and progress on their journeys.

Garth Brooks said it so well in his song, "Unanswered Prayers". Sometimes we should give thanks for things not going as we want them to. Sometimes 'God' – or maybe our subconscious or soul – knows better, and we get to the path we are supposed to be on in spite of ourselves.

Laura decided to follow her dream to be a travel representative. To her surprise she was chosen over hundreds of younger, more qualified women. She is still married and has decided to wait and see how that plays out. Maybe their relationship will last.

Or maybe...

You did figure out that Laura's husband, who was Sebastien, is Jessica, didn't you?

...maybe Jessica, will be able to finally move on and follow her own dreams.

Maybe that was the plan all along. To help Jacob understand *and* Jessica to move on.

CHAPTER 12:

NOW WHAT?

There are so many more fascinating stories to be told, but my biggest wish is that this book inspires you to find your own.

Each of us has things we want to experience, people we want to be with, and lessons we want to learn. We all have our own goals and agendas to achieve them, but sometimes we get stuck.

Sometimes we get into a cycle we repeat over and over. Each time we try to change a few things to break the cycle, to learn the lesson, but sometimes it takes lifetimes to achieve it.

Don't give up. Explore, question, and analyze. Look for patterns in your life. Find the connections. Don't accept being stuck repeating the same things over and over, life after life.

If you use the help of a hypnotist, hypnotherapist, or psychic, the important part is what *you* learn and how you apply it to *your* life.

There are numerous resources to investigate. From books on the subconscious and hypnosis, to ones on reincarnations and past lives. More and more therapists are delving into these areas to help their clients. Talk to people, you might be surprised how many others are looking for the same insight you are.

We live in an age that allows these types of journeys, a time where we are not burned at the stake for our differences or tortured for speaking out. We are allowed to be free thinkers, free to express ourselves and explore.

So be a free thinker. Express yourself, and explore everything life has to offer!

Learn those hidden lessons. Find your life's purpose.

APPENDIX

WORKSHEETS: GETTING STARTED

To help you begin your journey, I have included some worksheets to get you thinking in the right direction. For an electronic copy visit my website at http://insight4success.ca
or e-mail me directly at lynn@insight4success.ca

EXERCISE 1:
– YOUR BELIEFS –

Beliefs can block the retrieval
of past life information.

- *The purpose of this exercise is to help you identify your beliefs regarding reincarnation and the concept of past lives.*
- *This is an individual and very personal exercise – it is your beliefs we are trying to find.*
- *There are no correct answers.*

Note: *The only way to get past blocks is to address your specific belief and fears.*

Why do people exist? What is the purpose of life?
_____
_____
_____
_____
_____
_____
_____
_____

The Portal To Past Life Insight

Why do people go through bad times?

What happens when someone does something bad, on a soul level?

What do we bring forwards from past lives?

Is it alright to see a past life? Why? Why not?

Do you have any fears about seeing your past lives?

EXERCISE 2:
– PATTERNS IN YOUR LIFE –

Repetitive situations represent lessons
your soul is working on.

- *The purpose of this exercise is to help you identify reoccurring patterns in your life. Which in turn, can help you see what your soul is trying to learn?*
- *There are some benefits of doing this exercise with others. Sometimes other people can see our patterns more easily because they are not as close to the situation as we are.*
- *The patterns you are looking for are things that were not pleasant. Pleasant things we often forget, unpleasant things we tend to remember. This is how the subconscious helps us learn.*

Look at your love life, any unsettling things that keep happening?

_____
_____
_____
_____
_____
_____
_____

Look at your relationship with your parents, anything that bugs you?

Look at your relationship with your children, how do they push your buttons?

Look at your jobs, any similarities between the ones you hated?

The Portal To Past Life Insight

Look at your health, any reoccurring issues?

_____
_____
_____
_____
_____
_____
_____

Are some of your answers similar among these groups? Is there an issue or scenario that could be said for multiple questions?

_____
_____
_____
_____
_____
_____
_____

Pick one of these patterns and a specific incident. (The most irritating works well.) Describe what happened.

_____
_____
_____
_____
_____
_____
_____

How did you feel? Be as detailed in your feelings as possible.

How do you feel looking back at this incident?

EXERCISE 3:
– ACCESSING YOUR SUBCONSCIOUS –

This process can reveal key
information from your subconscious.

- *This exercise should be done in private with time to explore.*
- *Do this exercise with your feelings. Always check in with how you felt or feel, and write that down as well.*
- *There are no wrong or dumb answers.*
- *Don't **think** about the answers just let your ideas flow.*
- *Don't force the answers. If nothing comes leave that question for another time.*
- *Don't analyze or edit as you go, you can do that later.*

Note: You might be surprise at what comes up.

Review your last two answers in Exercise 2. Were there any other times in your life you felt this way?

_____
_____
_____
_____
_____
_____

Are there other times in your life that remind you of this event? Why?

Why do you think these things keep coming up in your life?

If it was to learn something, what would that be?
(Remember it is never the easy answer. Look deeper.)

EXERCISE 4:
– POSSIBLE PAST LIVES –

There are clues in our daily
life about our past lives.

- *The purpose of this exercise is to identify locations or themes that have bled through from previous lives.*
- *This exercise is another fun one to do with family or friends.*
- *Take each question as deep as you can go. Continue to ask the five Ws and H questions – who, what, where, when, why, and how. Especially push the **why**. Why do you think or feel that?*

Where have you always wanted to go? Why?

_____
_____
_____
_____
_____
_____
_____

Where wouldn't you go, even if it was free? Why?

What periods in history do you like to learn about? Consider time period and location / country.

Do you have any phobias or fears? Why?

What are your favorite movies or books? Why?

Do you have any pet peeves? Why?

EXERCISE 5:
– FINDING SOMEONE TO HELP –

Hypnotist, Hypnotherapist, Medium, or Psychic.

- Regardless of where you go, there are common questions you should ask.
- Always remember this is your journey and should be at your pace.
- Don't be forced into something. Use your feelings to tell you if what they say fits *you*.

Look beyond credentials.
1. Do they specialize in regression, specifically past lives?
2. Do they have references?
3. If you were referred by a friend, do you trust that friend in this area?
4. Do they offer a consult?
5. Do they provide a recording of their sessions?

Find the proper person for you.
1. Do you trust them exploring your subconscious? (All of them do.)
2. Were you given time to get to know them? Or will you be given that time?
3. How do you feel in their presence?

4. Do they act like a facilitator or guide? Or are they more pushy?
5. Are they doing this for entertainment or for another reason? Ask them to explain why they think exploring past lives is important.

Always go with your gut feelings.

If for any reason you feel uncomfortable – stop, even if you are in the middle of a session.

Remember what they say can impact your life.

ABOUT THE AUTHOR

Lynn LeBlanc is passionate about assisting individuals on their soul's journey. In addition to her Certified Clinical Hypnotherapy designation, she also has a bachelor degree in commerce and education. This training has created a perfect blend for helping clients identify, understand, and overcome challenges in all aspects of their lives. She teaches adult classes about the subconscious mind and the relevance of past lives on current life issues. In addition, Lynn's strong problem-solving background allows her to explore multiple lives and analyze information retrieved using an innovative new process. This process provides a different perspective that empowers individuals to find understanding and happiness.

Recently Lynn revisited her enthusiasm for writing and completed her first book, *The Portal to Past Live Insight*. She is working on her next two books, *The Portal to Finding Life Lessons* and *The Portal to Discovering Life's Purpose*.

Lynn also operates her own hypnotherapy practice called Insight 4 Success Inc., http://www.insight4success.ca.

Look for
Lynn C. LeBlanc's
-- Next Book --

THE PORTAL
TO
FINDING LIFE LESSONS

Coming Soon!